MOMENTUM
MASTERS

MOMENTUM MASTERS

A Roundtable Interview with Super Traders

**Mark Minervini, Dan Zanger,
David Ryan, and Mark Ritchie II**

Access Publishing Group, LLC
Accesspubgroup@gmail.com

ISBN 978-0-9963079-0-1 (pbk)

ISBN 978-0-9963079-1-8 (ebk)

Printed in the United States of America

First Edition

10 9 8 7 6 5 4 3 2 1

Contents

The Why and How of This Book

Throughout his career, Mark Minervini has been approached by countless traders, from novices to veterans, with questions about how to achieve success in the stock market. Many of these knowledge seekers learned about Mark when he won the U.S. Investing Championship in 1997, or later when they read about him in Jack Schwager's bestselling book *Stock Market Wizards: Interviews with America's Top Stock Traders*.

Since then, Mark's trading fame has exploded with the 2013 publication of his first book, *Trade Like a Stock Market Wizard: How to Achieve Superperformance in Stocks* (McGraw-Hill). A distillation of wisdom gained from Mark's 30 years of trading high-momentum stocks, *Trade Like a Stock Market Wizard* became an immediate bestseller among investment titles and sparked a huge following, including more than 100,000 Twitter followers. Three-time U.S. Investing Champion David Ryan declared *Trade Like a Stock Market Wizard* to be "the most comprehensive work I have ever read on investing in growth stocks."

Despite its depth and breadth, *Trade Like a Stock Market Wizard* stoked rather than satiated traders' hunger for knowledge. In the two years following the book's publication, readers flooded the office of Minervini Private Access with nearly a thousand questions. Some queries delved further into topics covered in the book, while others sought to explore new territory. It dawned on us that Mark's readers—including many of you reading this now—had entrusted us with a real treasure trove. Drawing on their own hard-earned trading experiences, readers collectively had furnished us with an incredibly detailed and wide-ranging inventory of the real-world challenges and knowledge gaps confronting traders.

We then asked a question of our own: How should we respond to this windfall? I suggested to Mark that he answer many of these questions in a book. Mark replied, "I have an even better idea. Why don't we ask some of the best stock traders I know to answer these questions with me?" Mark reached out to his friends David Ryan, Dan Zanger, and Mark Ritchie II, three of the most successful stock traders in America. They enthusiastically agreed to participate, and project *Momentum Masters* was under way.

Momentum Masters takes a unique approach. We chose 130 of the most relevant questions submitted to our office and organized them by category into related sections. I want to emphasize that these questions were submitted by real traders confronting real issues in the stock market. There are no questions based on our opinions or ideas of what traders might be interested in knowing. The format of *Momentum Masters* also parts company from most trader interview books in a fundamental way. Instead of dividing the interviews into separate chapters for each market master, Mark, David, Dan, and

Mark II answer each question in a roundtable format, allow-ing the reader to compare and contrast.

Now if I may, let me give you a heads-up before you dive in.

First, *Momentum Masters* offers no colorful biographi-cal details, literary flourishes, or other diversions with which many market books, including some excellent ones, try to "spice up" or lighten the material. This book is all meat; ques-tions and answers all pertain to trading.

Second, as you read through the questions and answers, take note of the differences as well as the common character-istics among the four masters. As I said, the format was chosen deliberately to facilitate comparisons. David Ryan, a 40-year trading veteran, and Mark Minervini, with more than 30 years' trading experience, favor fast-growing small- and mid-cap stocks. Dan Zanger, a 25-year trader, prefers the larger-cap stocks and even mega-cap names. Mark Ritchie II, the youngest of the group, won the Triple-Digit Challenge at the first of the annual Mark Minervini Master Trader Program workshops in 2010. The challenge was to become the first attendee to return 100% using what was learned on his or her trading account. Ritchie II did it—achieving triple-digit performance—in less than six months. During the subsequent five years, Minervini has closely watched Ritchie deliver con-sistently superior trading performance. He told me, "Ritchie is a Momentum Master in the making and should be included in this book."

To succeed as a stock trader, you need to learn what to buy, when to buy, and when to sell. More importantly, you will need to match your own trading style to your psychology and strengths and learn how to improve your weaknesses. As you compare and contrast the answers to each question, keep a sharp eye for the fundamental practices and core principles that these traders share. These nuances are the similarities between highly successful Momentum Masters.

Through the diverse insights, acumen, and trading experiences of the four masters, readers will attain an education in trading like none other—and all grounded in the areas that interest them most. So there you have it. A plethora of knowledge now awaits you. Good reading and best of success on your own journey to greater returns with less risk.

Bob Weissman
Editor

Meet the Momentum Masters

MARK MINERVINI

Mark is the author of the bestselling book *Trade Like a Stock Market Wizard: How to Achieve Superperformance in Stocks in Any Market*. Starting with only a few thousand dollars, Mark turned his personal trading account into millions, averaging 220% per year for five consecutive years with only one losing quarter, achieving an incredible 36,000% total return. To put that in perspective, a $100,000 account would explode to over $30 million in just five years.

To demonstrate the capabilities of his SEPA® methodology, in 1997, Mark put up $250,000 of his own money and entered the U.S. Investing Championship. Trading against highly leveraged futures and options traders, Mark traded a long-only stock portfolio to win the real-money investment derby with a 155% annual return, a performance that was nearly double the nearest competing money manager.

Mark is featured in Jack Schwager's *Stock Market Wizards: Interviews with America's Top Stock Traders*. Schwager wrote: "Minervini's performance has been nothing short of astounding. Most traders and money managers would be delighted to have Minervini's worst year—a 128 percent gain—as their best."

Mark educates traders about his trading methodology through Minervini Private Access, a streaming communication platform that allows users the unique experience of trading side by side with him in real time. He also conducts a live Master Trader Program workshop, where he teaches his system in a two-day weekend event. You can learn more about Mark at www.minervini.com.

DAVID RYAN

David is a protégé of the legendary William O'Neil and a former money manager at William O'Neil & Co. After graduating college in 1982, David went to work for O'Neil's company, and within four years, he was appointed the youngest vice president and O'Neil's direct assistant responsible for money management and stock selection for the firm's institutional clients.

David won the U.S. Investing Championship three years in a row between 1985 and 1987. In 1985 he was up 161% and in 1986 an almost an identical 160%. He reentered the contest in 1987 and won for the third year in a row when he was up again over 100 percent. For the three years his total return was 1,379%.

David successfully ran a mutual fund for 5 years and his own hedge fund, Rustic Partners, for 15 years. He continues to actively trade his own investment account. David is featured in Jack Schwager's *Market Wizards: Interviews with*

Top Traders. Schwager wrote: "Although most of the traders I interview have a love for trading, none have the unbridled enthusiasm demonstrated by Ryan. I suspect that as long as he was supplied with his charts, he would probably be content to work in a hall closet."

DAN ZANGER

Dan is the chief technical analyst for the stock website chartpattern.com and author of the *The Zanger Report* newsletter. During the late 1990s, Dan turned $10,775 into an audited gain of $18 million in just 18 months. That's a 164,000% return.

As a former pool contractor, Dan first gained worldwide recognition for his trading achievements in an article that appeared in *Fortune Magazine* in December 2000 entitled "My Stocks Are Up 10,000%!" Dan spent 25 years devoting every spare moment to studying charts. Using chart patterns, Dan eventually developed a robust trading system that responds to all market conditions.

Dan was voted Top 100 Trader of the Year by *Trader Monthly Magazine* two years in a row. He has been featured in such publications as *Barron's, Forbes, Fortune, Active Trader, Trader Monthly,* and *Traders World* as well as been a guest on many radio and TV shows. He has been a frequent contributor to *Technical Analysis of Stocks & Commodities* magazine and *SFO* magazine. *Fortune* magazine referred to Dan's cockpit trading style as "a rock keyboardist surrounded by synthesizers."

MARK RITCHIE II

Mark is the son of the well-known Mark Ritchie (*Market Wizards, God in the Pits,* and *My Trading Bible*). Although a relative newcomer to the investment world, Ritchie II is a potent addition to the *Momentum Masters* all-star lineup. He achieved a 100% return in less than six months to win Mark Minervini's 2010 Triple-Digit Challenge. Since then, Ritchie's account is up 540%; in 2014 alone, he was up 110%. His total return since 2010 has exceeded 1,000%

Ritchie II manages a pool of his own capital together with friends and family through RTM2, LLC. He has a degree in philosophy from Illinois State and currently resides in the Chicago suburbs with his wife and five children.

SECTION ONE

Introduction

S1-1: Each of you has been trading for a long time. Do you trade the same way and rely on the same chart patterns that you did earlier in your career? Or have times changed and so has your trading style accordingly?

Minervini: I've refined things a bit and added some new techniques, but 95% is unchanged. That's the beauty of supply and demand; it's timeless. The only thing I do more of is trade pullback setups, and that's just because I developed new pullback buy techniques and got better at it. But my trading approach has remained virtually unchanged for over three decades.

Ryan: Yes, I am still buying the same chart patterns I did when I first started. I have added a few nuances to my trading style. While I still buy breakouts, I also buy pullbacks in strong stocks. Earlier in my career I only bought breakouts. These days many stocks break out, pull back, then start a move higher.

Zanger: The same chart patterns that are in the market today were evident 100 years ago, and I suspect they will be here for many more years to come. So, yes, I trade the same way today as I did 20 years ago, and I think it's safe to say I will be trading the same way 20 years from now. I will say that I'm far better at cashing out of stocks before a market breaks or a significant downdraft occurs than I was 5 years ago.

Ritchie II: Well, I can't comment on the nature of major changes to my trading from many years ago, as I haven't been around for decades as these other fellows have been. But I will say that I track my trades as diligently as I follow charts, so I can see trends in my trading. What I can tell you is that I've certainly noticed that there are often different technical themes within certain market periods. For example, lately it has been very difficult to buy new 52-week or all-time-high–type breakouts, whereas other times it has been much easier. Some of this undoubtedly has to do with where we're at in the overall cycle and how obvious or more failure prone some types of breakouts can become.

S1-2: What about your daily routine—has it changed or evolved over time?

Minervini: Like my trading techniques, my routine is relatively unchanged as well. Most of my work is done the night before, so when the market opens, I already know the stocks I'm interested in and at what price levels. I get in front of my trading screen at 8:30 a.m. ET. The first thing I do is look at earnings released and news items that may affect my holdings, and I also look at premarket futures to get an idea of how the market will open. I then review all my current holdings and update my stops and set alerts; I set audio alerts on my buy candidates at price levels near my target purchase price and also at levels near my sell stops.

Everything I do is thought out; I don't like surprises, so I try to work out as much as possible in advance so I don't get blindsided and caught off guard. I do this work outside of market hours to remove emotion. When trading in real time, things can get very emotional, so the more you can work out in advance, the easier it will be to take action when under fire. The only thing different from when I first started is the computer, which I didn't have 30 years ago; I plotted charts by hand on graph paper, if you can imagine that.

Ryan: My daily routine consists of getting up an hour before the market opens (I am on the West Coast, so it's hard to get up much earlier). I spend time reading the Bible to get my perspective and to keep focus on what is really important. I then go over the news on the market and specific stocks. I have already prepared a watch list and set alerts the previous day after the close. I usually don't do much in the first 45 minutes of trading because there are many false moves and reactions to overnight news.

Zanger: My daily routine is the same now as it was 25 years ago. I start the day off watching the premarket ticker tape on CNBC with the sound off and get a feel for the stocks crossing the tape. Then I take a look at stock futures and get some coffee brewing and turn on the monitors. I fire up my IQXP.com Sounds of the Market program I had written 15 years ago and literally hear which stocks are popping on the bid or the ask.

As soon as the market opens, I want to see how stocks are moving; are they gapping up with no volume, in which case they will likely sell down right away. Or are they gapping down on light volume, in which case it's a buying opportunity to add to some positions. Gapping up or down on heavy volume tells me they are likely to extend from there.

Ritchie II: My routine basically breaks down into two categories: (1) pre-trading and post-trading, which consists of about two hours before and after each trading day, and (2) the trading day itself. The pre-trading–post-trading routine is similar to watching a game film before the game. One of my football coaches used to always tell me, "You've got to read and know your keys so the speed of the game slows down, which takes you to where the action is rather than chasing it down from behind." That's what my pre-trading–post-trading routine does for me.

I know what and where I'm going to buy before the market opens, so there are no surprises, and I just act without thinking. I start in the morning by checking all my open positions. Then I check where the general market is trading as well as the U.S. bond futures. I review my watch list and set alarms on any stocks that I believe are actionable. From that list, I determine if there are any stocks that I actually may purchase, and I calculate exactly how many shares I would be buying.

Throughout the day I watch all the stocks on my watch list as well as the S&P and U.S. bond futures. If it's a particularly slow day where I don't have many prospective buys, I will often look at other charts or do market research on anything that interests me. I'm always a continuing student of the markets.

After the market closes, I run through daily screens of anywhere from 200 to 500 charts of individual stocks to compile a series of watch lists. I then look through my watch lists as well as screen for actionable ideas. I also log any and all trades from the previous trading day in a strategy-specific manner.

S1-3: How do you feel about high-frequency trading (HFT)?

Minervini: I think it's absurd that this practice is allowed, and it should be addressed more seriously. The U.S. stock market needs to be a fair and even playing field. HFT is a step in the wrong direction. It's a loophole that allows front-running.

Ryan: I don't like it at all. As Mark said and as described in a *60 Minutes* broadcast in 2014, high-frequency trading is front-running, which is illegal. It also tends to create a lot of noise and false moves. I wouldn't mind if the stock exchanges brought back the uptick rule and even specialists to keep a much more orderly market. Even with all the noise, stocks still move higher on earnings or the expectation of higher earnings.

Zanger: I have found that since HFT entered the picture in 2001, there is a lot more choppiness during the day, which I believe is designed to shake us out of our stocks. The introduction of decimals from eighths has allowed HFT to come on strong since the spread is so narrow now. Combine these high-frequency algorithms with rapidly evolving artificial intelligence that only gets more sophisticated and subtle with time; we human traders must accept it and adapt accordingly.

For instance, by buying intraday weakness and using faster time frames such as three- or five-minute charts. Or alternatively, you can end-run the whole HFT quagmire by buying breakouts from solid bases and letting those winners run for a few months. HFT is largely irrelevant then.

On a closing note about volatility and choppiness, we can't completely blame HFT. The advent of online stock trading brought in tens of thousands of retail traders buying and selling with great frequency that added to the energy and sensitivity of the marketplace. And let's not forget the e-mini futures contracts that began in October 1997. In my opinion this really started some of the wildest swings in the market because this new e-mini contract brought in thousands of newly minted traders trying their hand at futures tied to the S&P 500. It goes without saying that the easy access afforded by online trading platforms was a fundamental shift that aided the volatility.

Ritchie II: I have many strong opinions on this subject, the first of which is that HFT has never been adequately defined and ought to be. We cannot have a well-informed understanding or debate about it until it's well defined; and many in opposition to HFT don't have a good working definition of what it is they are opposing.

For example, the head of one of the largest equity exchanges got caught in an argument on television saying that his firm matched trades using direct market feeds, when in fact the firm didn't. The exchange spokespeople tried to defuse the situation later, but the head guy either lied or didn't know how trades on his own exchange were being processed, and the media and regulators gave him a pass with no follow-up . . . nothing.

That said, it is my belief—and I think it has been fairly well documented—that there are certain practices in the HFT world that are legal yet highly unethical. For example, in the old days of the trading floors and pits, if you went and looked at a clerk or runner's order and then outran him to the pit in order to bid the market up or down in anticipation of those orders, you would be thrown off the floor, fined, or worse.

Likewise, if you tried to bully the market by jamming huge sizes on the offer or bid, you couldn't then step out of the way if someone yelled "Sold"; you couldn't then turn around and say "Oh, I changed my size from 1,000 to 10" as you were yelling "Sold." However, in both cases this is precisely what we have taking place today in many of our equity and futures exchanges. The market ought to be a mechanism for fair and orderly price discovery, and many of the games that some of these firms are playing undermine the very spirit of what the markets are here for.

S1-4: How did you originally get into trading; what was the attraction? And what has kept you motivated over the years?

Minervini: I originally got interested in trading because I grew up poor and I wanted to get rich. I saw the market as the ultimate opportunity for riches without prejudices—it's just you and the market—and if you're good, you get rich. Although once I started trading, the challenge became more intriguing than the money; the money became just a way to keep score. I would probably still be trading today even if I had not become wealthy from it. I simply love the art of speculation; I don't see myself walking away from trading regardless of how much money I have made or will make in the future.

More recently, teaching my approach to others and hearing their success stories is really gratifying, and it motivates me to continue sharing my own knowledge. Interestingly, about 26 years ago I went to see David Ryan speak at a seminar, and now he's here with me in a book, and we also work together instructing at seminars. Mark Ritchie II came to my workshop in 2010, and here he is as a young successful trader sharing his insights with us.

Ryan: My dad started buying stocks for me for my college education when I started elementary school. At the dinner table he would discuss why he bought different companies. I bought my first stock at age 13 in a candy company called Wards Foods, which made Bit O' Honey and Chunky candy bars. From there I became fascinated about why my stock went down and others went up. To me, it was like a treasure hunt, looking through thousands of companies searching for those two or three stocks that would turn out to be the superperformers.

Zanger: My mom used to watch the business channel KWHY-TV, channel 22, on UHF back in the mid-1970s. This channel provided the first ticker tape on TV in the country, and she loved to sit in front of the TV and read the *LA Times* and listen to the business news throughout the day. I would come home from school and watch that ticker tape running and listen to the technical guys talking stocks and commodities, but I couldn't figure out what they were talking about most of the time. However, I was fascinated with the ticker tape at the bottom of the screen.

One day out of the blue, one symbol started to dominate the tape, and it was going by at $1, and I knew I wanted in on that one. I raced down to Kennedy, Cabot & Co. in Beverly Hills and opened a brokerage account for $1,000, and I bought 1,000 shares of this cheap stock. About three or four weeks later, the stock was at $3.50. I sold it, and I've been hooked on stocks ever since.

Ritchie II: I come from a trading family, so to speak; my father and several of my uncles were all successful floor traders in Chicago. So you could say it was in my genes, although I've never traded from the floor and I wasn't all that interested in trading growing up, as most of my family was retired or on to other ventures by the time I became interested.

After I graduated from college, I worked for a former trader of my father's for a summer, just placing orders, looking at charts, etc., and I really enjoyed it. A couple of years later, he offered me a job, sort of being his trading assistant in the hopes of eventually having a larger prop shop or starting a fund. While there, I traded for him, some on his behest and some on my own. During this time, my curiosity for what makes markets tick and how to become a good trader was really piqued.

I remain motivated based on my desire to continually improve, as I don't believe I have "arrived" in terms of my trading potential and performance.

S1-5: Were you successful right away, or did you go through tough times? How long did it take for you to become consistently profitable?

Minervini: In the beginning, I made all types of mistakes. It took me a while to learn the important lessons, mostly by trial and error. I produced terrible results for about six years. I became consistently profitable when I finally said to myself, "The heck with my ego; the goal is to make money, not be right." Once I decided to put my ego aside, admit my mistakes, and cut my losses and protect profits, then the big performance and the consistency started coming together.

Ryan: When I really got started, just out of college, I doubled an account and then lost it all and then some. I then studied all the mistakes I had made and became extremely disciplined, and then I became much more successful. That process took over two years. Like anything else, it takes time to get good, and you usually have to make a lot of mistakes before you get the hang of it. It starts with the right method, the right money management, a very small ego so you can admit mistakes, and a tremendous amount of discipline to be successful in the markets.

Zanger: Eventually I got serious about stocks and came up with $100,000 in 1991 and got a huge satellite dish on my roof for real-time quotes using BMI and Live-Wire for charts. Neither of these two companies exists in these formats today. The Gulf War had just started, and the market soared. I quickly turned that $100,000 into $440,000, and I thought

I was on the road to riches beyond my wildest dreams. Then I got my first experience of a market correction, and that $440,000 quickly became $220,000.

I spent the next six years trying to get that $220,000 back to $440,000, but all I did was get crushed from one stock to the next; and before I knew it, I was broke and actually ended up owing my broker $225 due to the market break in October 1997.

I had no more cash to put in the market, so I had to sell one of my cars to raise cash to get started again. I sold it for $11,000 and deposited that into my brokerage account, which covered my debt of $225 and left me with $10,775 to trade. It also left me so angry that I swore to myself that those bastards would never get my cash again. I was never going to let a belief blind me and get in the way of a trade again. I said to myself, "If a stock gets very shaky for even a single day, I'm out." I would trust no stock blindly ever again, and I knew that anything I might read during the market day is intended to mislead me from the winning side of the trade.

The next thing I knew, the Internet bubble hit, and I have never looked back again. But I must admit that it was that string of losses that turned the tide for me; it completely revamped how I thought and how I traded. I never believed in a stock's story, or a rumor, or a news report ever again. Everything I need to know is based on the stock's price behavior and volume; the rest is pure noise.

Ritchie II: I certainly was not successful right away. I naively thought I would be, but I learned quickly that I had some good ideas but needed to refine them as well as myself in order to be successful. I'd be lying if I said that I wasn't tempted to think about quitting more than a few times in my first year. I should also be transparent and say that I don't in any way feel that I've arrived as a trader or am even worthy of inclusion in this book. That being said, I just about broke even during my first year and, on a risk-adjusted basis, have done better every year since. The year 2014 was my best in terms of total return and return relative to risk. I went from not knowing what I was doing to a pretty good understanding of risk, and my returns and income grew along the way.

S1-6: Do the big players have an edge over the individual investor? How do you respond to comments that the game is rigged?

Minervini: The game is not rigged! In fact, the small individual investor has a huge advantage over the big mutual fund or hedge fund manager, mainly due to liquidity and speed. Think of it as the large institution driving a cruise ship and the small trader behind the wheel of a speedboat. Who do you think would outmaneuver whom?

In my experience, those who say the game is rigged are those who haven't been able to outperform the market, so they feel it's unbeatable. It's not rigged! In the stock market, you can make money or you can make excuses, but you can't make both. So stop making excuses and start making money. That starts with accepting the fact that you can beat the market if you really want to. But you have to first accept that not only is the market beatable, but you yourself can do it in a big way.

Ryan: It would take too much money to rig the largest financial market in the world. That is just an excuse for underperformance and is a sign that someone has given up. The big players have an advantage in that they have access to more and better information. They also pay a lot for that information. But they also have much more capital to invest, and so it is harder to move around. If the individual investor can train his eye to spot institutional buying, he can move faster and take advantage of getting in front of some of that buying.

Zanger: The "size" knife cuts both ways. The little guys can get in and out of trades far easier than the big players. However, the big guys routinely shake out the little guy with all the media power at their fingertips. Hype and lies are favorite tools of the larger players. The little guys are left grasping at straws as they buy too high, hold losers for too long, buy on the way down, or buy into rumors at inflated prices. These behaviors are all encouraged and carefully engineered by the big boys.

Ritchie II: I would start by saying that "rigged" has become a catchphrase that is highly ambiguous and misleading. I would say that almost all traders, including the big players, are at a disadvantage to the current structure and market-making situation, based on everything I've experienced, seen, and studied.

That said, the market makers don't drive the ultimate direction of the market. They may screw and jerk around short-term moves and individual executions, but if a market is going to move, then big funds and institutions are going to drive it. The bigger players have to buy and sell often during days or even weeks. Individual traders have a significant advantage over the big traders, because individual traders can move in and out of positions much faster. So they can change direction very quickly when market conditions change, and to me, that's a tremendous edge.

S1-7: Do you think an individual with a full-time job can successfully trade stocks by using only the end-of-the-day pricing?

Minervini: Yes, but it's going to be more difficult to track your trades and place orders, so you may have to rely on mechanical stops. Luckily, the trading platforms nowadays are very powerful and offer a host of options.

Ryan: Yes. Sitting in front of a computer screen all day, watching the action, might sound like fun, but I have found it can also be a detriment to one's performance. My biggest winners occurred when I held for the intermediate to long term. For me, it's better to concentrate on the longer-term picture and not get caught up with intraday trading. Sometimes a move on a 10-minute chart can look so scary; but when you step back, it's very minor when viewed on a daily or even weekly time frame. There have been too many times when I have been shaken out of a good position by looking at the short-term time frame. To me, the big money is made in the longer-term moves.

Zanger: There are many that do well trading stocks on top of full-time jobs today. Smartphones have moved us to a whole new level. Naturally when you can't trade in real time and watch every tick, you must be far more selective in choosing stocks that match your trading style. But I remember my own days in the pool business holding a Quotrek, an early wireless device introduced around 1983 that delivered real-time streaming quotes and news, in one hand and grasping the steering wheel of a truck in the other. I wouldn't be where I am today without that determination to trade no matter what.

Ritchie II: If by successful you mean get a market-beating risk-adjusted return over time, then I highly doubt it. If you mean picking a few good stocks for their portfolio that will do well over time from a longer time horizon, then I think that the individual probably can, although few probably do.

S1-8: If you're not able to be in front of your computer during the trading day, what would be your method to enter and exit trades?

Minervini: You can enter stops with your broker, and you can use bracket orders. Today, there are many algorithms offered on trading platforms that make it easier than ever.

Ryan: Stops. I would set buy and sell stops the night before. In doing that, you avoid the distraction of the market and might be able to make good, unemotional decisions.

Zanger: I think the smartphone and a leading quote screen provided by a number of brokerage houses are all you need. This will show you volume and price quickly, and then you can tab over to a chart if needed.

Ritchie II: Well, if I wasn't in front of my screen, I would probably have to trade from a longer time horizon in most situations. Having said that, I would still use some kind of intraday stop protection to ensure against a very large decline.

S1-9: Do you ever use margin or options to leverage your trades?

Minervini: Not anymore. I used to use margin when I first started trading. I traded options early on, but I feel there's too much working against you with options.

Ryan: I rarely use options. I don't like the time decay. If the stock just goes sideways, the time value will erode, and the option can expire worthless. I like to concentrate on doing one thing well and not try all kinds of instruments. I use margin only when the market is in a nice uptrend without a lot of volatility, and even then, it is only when all my stocks are doing well.

Zanger: At times I use margin, and maybe once a year I'll find a stock worth trying some calls on. Both instances have to be the right stock at the right time, or one can get smoked very badly. I always tell people that I never really started to make money in stocks until I quit trading, or better said, playing with options. Rookies love options, which is why they stay rookies.

Ritchie II: I use margin only when I'm having success on the heels of profits from being fully invested. If I'm fully invested and things are working great, and now I want to use those gains to buy more shares, then I go on margin. I only do it by pyramiding the whole portfolio up the same way I would a winning position. I only trade options in specific situations where I think they offer a better risk-reward than the underlying stock. Also, this is usually in very liquid names or in a situation where I think there's a chance we could get a very rapid move.

S1-10: Do you think trading at a really high level requires a natural-born talent, or can the skills be learned? How long is the typical learning curve?

Minervini: I think trading is no different from sports. There are some people that have genetic advantages (for example, muscularity, agility, etc.); however, that alone doesn't determine the ultimate outcome. There are geniuses that don't succeed in life and naturally talented athletes that go nowhere. And then you have individuals that started out disadvantaged, like I did, but they succeed at a high level.

As far as the learning curve is concerned, there's good news. As a result of the Internet and social media, you have access to a plethora of information previously not available. As long as you can sort through the BS and differentiate the wheat from the chaff, you have access to some very valuable people who can help really compress the time it takes to learn how to trade correctly.

Make no mistake; nothing beats real-life experience—that's something you can't force—and it takes time to gain experience. Generally speaking, I would say the learning curve is at least a few years up to maybe five years, depending on how much time and attention you give to your trading.

Ryan: Trading at a high level requires that a number of things be done correctly, and that takes certain personality characteristics. You need to be extremely disciplined, focused, and humble and be willing to learn and take risk. If you lack any one of those characteristics, you can still get decent returns but probably not triple-digit returns consistently.

Most of the skills required can be learned, but if you lack the courage to take risk, it will be hard to make a purchase when the stock moves through its buy point. Or if you have a big ego and think you are right and the market is wrong, you can set yourself up for a very big loss. I have found the learning curve takes about two years, and it could take longer if you have to correct some bad habits. You usually have to make a lot of mistakes, learn from them, and then start making the right moves.

Zanger: It requires certain natural-born abilities, but the rest has to be learned. I've had more than two dozen friends and acquaintances watch me trade during the past 18 years, and one person above the others seemed to naturally grasp what I was seeing in the charts and was able to get the gist of things at an instinctive level quickly. Unfortunately, this person was young and still felt the need to go off to college, which left no funds or time to master the art of trading. In time this individual might come back to it, and I hope she does, as she was able to read the charts with relative ease.

As far as the learning curve, that really depends on the intensity of the commitment. Are you watching the market every day on a real-time feed or just peeking at the market a few times a day? If I had to put a number on it, I would say the exceptional trader is working at it full-time for at least five years and experiencing at least one complete market cycle.

Ritchie II: I'm probably the best or worst person to answer this question, depending upon how you look at it. That said, I am actually in the middle when it comes to the nature-versus-nurture debate. I believe that a natural aptitude for any endeavor is important but not necessarily essential. There is a degree to which an individual's drive, discipline, and motivation can override lack of talent. I honestly don't consider myself to be more talented or intelligent than the next guy, but I am blessed with a good memory and the ability to maintain discipline.

I certainly think an average person can learn enough to be adequate; to say that everyone can trade at a high level though is probably misleading. In regard to the time it takes to learn, I would defer to Tony Robbins, who says that "most people overestimate what they can do in two years and underestimate what they can do in ten years." Somewhere between two and ten years, people will either learn the skills necessary to succeed or probably give up.

S1-11: Is it still possible to get rich trading stocks even if you start with a small account?

Minervini: Absolutely! There are still great opportunities, and there will be many more in the years to come. The commissions are low, and the access to available information has made for a very level playing field. It's a great time to be a stock trader.

Ryan: Definitely. The power of compounding gains over a number of years is enormous. But you can't do it all in one year. The key is executing your method correctly and not focusing on your equity value. If you work hard, learn from your mistakes, and stay disciplined, the gains will take care of themselves.

Zanger: Not only am I sure that it is, but I would recommend starting out small rather than large for all new traders. Bottom line, if you hone your timing and talent to spot the setups and if you have the fortitude to stick to the rules, it doesn't matter if you start out small; you have a true edge that few traders possess, especially if you do your homework every night and on weekends. I wouldn't be here if that weren't true.

Ritchie II: This all depends upon what your definition of "rich" is. I don't consider myself rich; however, I've been able to take a relatively small account and grow it pretty nicely, earn a good living, and make great risk-adjusted gains. So in that sense, I'm very rich. However, I haven't reached my longer-term goals yet. I wouldn't be trading if I didn't believe the stock market offered the opportunity to grow capital nicely. So, yes, of course it's possible.

SECTION TWO

Stock Selection

S2-1: What is the best way to find momentum stocks with big potential?

Minervini: I require that the stocks show strong relative price strength with high alpha and low standard deviation *before* I buy. One of the first books I read on the subject of relative strength (RS) was *The Relative Strength Concept* by Robert Levy. You can screen the market for strong RS stocks with many of the tools that are readily available today; there are free tools as well as paid subscription platforms.

Ryan: I would like to change that question to finding growth stocks, because I will not buy a stock just because it is going up. The stock has to be acting well in the market and have an earnings profile of the greatest winning stocks of all time. The source I use the most is MarketSmith followed by *Investor's Business Daily*. Both sources are designed to help you find the best growth stocks. They both provide numerous screens and lists for you to zero in on the best stocks.

Zanger: Price action is everything to me. Show me the big movers, and I'll show you a stock I want to own. Of course,

I'll be stealthy about it and look for a specific setup before considering it. I might even have to wait a few months before I jump into a strong mover with the right setup. Remember, these momentum stocks are temperamental and can go against you just as fast if you buy them at the wrong time.

One mistake I see over and over again is rookie traders buying a stock that is already up $10 on the day. Their emotions get the better of them, and the urge to jump in overwhelms them. They believe resolutely that the stock can go nowhere but to the stratosphere in the next few days. A few hard reversals, and these traders are gone—and blaming the cruel vicissitudes of the market when they should just take responsibility for their own lack of restraint.

Ritchie II: The best situations in my opinion often look the scariest. Meaning they have had a rapid price advance and look expensive. Relative strength is one way to find these kinds of situations; the higher the RS, the better.

S2-2: Do you have a minimum amount of volume for the stocks that you are trading?

Minervini: Yes, although for me it's pretty low. I often trade stocks that only trade 100,000–300,000 shares per day and even as low as 50,000 shares per day. You shouldn't be afraid of thinly traded stocks; you should embrace them. Some of the biggest winners are small companies that you've never heard of before. But you have to be careful and only trade a position size you can get out of safely.

A small position is better than no position, especially if the stock has the potential to skyrocket. This means that if the stock trades only 50,000 shares per day, I have to adjust my normal position size to accommodate. But a small position in a small stock that makes a big move is better than a big position in a liquid stock that goes nowhere. I've made most of my money in relatively smaller names.

Ryan: The stock usually has to trade at least 100,000 shares a day, or I avoid it.

Zanger: I try to stay with stocks that do at least 2 million shares a day or more. It's very hard to sell 100,000 shares or more of a stock when it breaks down due to a downgrade or a general market plunge. Even stocks that trade higher at 2 million to 4 million shares a day can have extreme volume or liquidity "dry-ups" at times.

Nothing is worse than becoming your own worst enemy as your own selling sends the stock down and no one wants to buy the stock on the heels of bad news or a downgrade. Every 1,000 shares you sell can cause the price to tank another $0.50 to $1 as you chip out.

I remember an occasion that I bought Baidu Inc. (BIDU) on a breakout in mid-September 2007, and it ran from $212 to over $360 in just three weeks. I held over 60,000 shares at the time, and some firm downgraded the stock when it was in this $360 area, and it started dropping right at the open. I thought this downgrade was going to take it down about $10, but it quickly surpassed that and was eventually down

$17 with no buyers in sight. I said to myself, "This is not good," and I started unloading shares quickly. The stock was down another $5 before I got out completely, but it eventually finished the day down a whopping $60! I can't tell you how happy I was to have sold way before being down that $60.

Now remember this stock was trading 2 million to 3 million shares a day prior to this sell-off, and I still got smoked. I have many other instances of heavy sell-offs, but the important point here is to adjust your position size to the average daily volume that the stock trades in case you need to get out quickly.

Ritchie II: I usually don't trade names that don't trade at least 25,000 shares a day on average.

S2-3: Have "dark pools" changed the way you analyze volume?

Minervini: No. Although volume could be skewed a bit intra-day and affect extrapolation, all volume data are included in the end-of-the-day tally, and that's the number I focus on the most.

Ryan: To me, volume is the lifeblood of a stock. Volume displays the basic supply and demand for a stock. Big stock movers are always powered by huge increases in volume. That big volume, as William O'Neil has always said, is "not your Aunt Suzy who lives down the street" but the mutual funds, hedge funds, and other big money managers powering the stock higher. Regardless of dark pools, the volume characteristics of big winners have not changed and are still showing up. If you don't learn how to analyze volume, you are missing a big portion of the technical picture.

Zanger: Volume is the mother's milk of momentum investing and is essential to price movement. The volume in dark pools is still factored in by the end of the day, so the total tally of shares can still be seen, albeit late. Personally, I have not noticed much impact by dark pools since they have come of age.

Ritchie II: Volume plays an important part in how I analyze a situation because I want to look for stocks that appear to be under accumulation, so I'm often looking for large up days on big volume, as well as decreasing volume on selling days. I don't see dark pools as being much of a factor in my analysis because I'm looking for the overall trend in volume behavior; and often I'm looking at the mid- to smaller-capitalized stocks, which don't have as heavy a dark pool participation.

S2-4: Do you ever bottom-fish?

Minervini: If you're asking if I try to pick a bottom when a stock is falling, the answer is no! However, I will buy a stock coming up off a normal pullback, but only if it's moving up through a pivot point and the stock is in a strong uptrend. I never try to catch falling knives. In my experience, it just leads to losses.

Ryan: I never buy new lows, if that is what you are asking.

Zanger: I catch a few muddy fish every now and again, but that is rare. All the biggest-moving stocks I've owned during the past 20 years, where I've made 95% of my money, were ones hitting new highs from very solid bases.

Ritchie II: Never in a momentum situation. I will from time to time scalp futures in what could be considered "bottom fishing," but only with very tight price and time stops.

S2-5: How about a price cutoff—do you buy low-priced stocks? If yes, do you treat them differently than you do higher-priced names?

Minervini: Most people think you need to invest in a low-priced stock to get in early and make a big gain. They think it's easier for a $1 stock to go to $2 than it is for a $30 stock to go to $60. Not true! But it is more likely that a $1 stock will go to zero. Using history as a guide, on average, the biggest winning stocks started their major advances above $30 a share.

Another mistake investors make is that they think it's better to own more shares, so they buy low-priced stocks. Just the opposite! I want to own the least number of shares; the more shares I own, the more of a liquidity issue I have. I prefer high-priced stocks—above $20–$30—versus low-priced stocks. Most of the time my cutoff is $12 per share—80% of my trades are in higher-priced names above $20–$30, which are more likely to attract institutional investors and support the stock with buying.

The severity of the bear market in 2008 created a proliferation of lower-priced names. Coming off that low, I traded more low-priced names than usual. However, low-priced stocks rarely make their way into my portfolio. When they do, I try to get in at the lowest-risk buy point possible because they tend to be more volatile than the higher-priced names.

Ryan: I rarely buy stocks below $15. The better-quality companies are usually higher priced. When I do buy a lower-priced stock, it is treated the same way as the rest of the stocks in my portfolio. Nothing should change just because the stock has a lower price.

Zanger: I find most cheap stocks are cheap for a reason, as they lack many of the characteristics I'm searching for in a stock. Also, if a $100 stock breaks out from a nice base and fails, I can then cut my loss at 3% or so, while a $10 stock that moves down $1 just cost me 10%. Higher-priced stocks tend to be very liquid and can make some nice $30–$50 gains in just a few weeks.

I rarely buy stocks under $70 a share, but I did buy a $2 stock recently. In November 2013, I bought this little biotech stock, Idera Pharmaceuticals Inc. (IDRA). I bought over 450,000 shares at around $2.20 or so, and it moved up to $6.60 in two months and then stalled out (see Chart 2.1). When it stalled out, I started unloading shares for a gain of about 120% net by the time I finished my selling.

That is probably my only success story that I can recall on stocks priced under $70 since the Internet bubble. I routinely bought stocks in the $40–$60 area then, though many were well over $70 up to $300.

Chart 2.1   Idera Pharmaceuticals Inc. (IDRA), 2013–2014

Ritchie II: For momentum trades, I only buy low-priced stocks that are liquid and in the highest 2–3% of relative strength. I also take smaller positions relative to my general exposure because the volatility in those names tends to be higher.

S2-6: Do you look for individual stocks from a "bottom-up" approach, or do you find a group that you see as leading first and then look for the individual stocks within the group?

Minervini: When I first started trading about three decades ago, I was a top-down investor. I would start with the general market and then look at the best groups and finally the stocks in those groups. What I found was that by the time the group was hot in a strong market, the best stocks had already blasted off. I was constantly missing the real market leaders that made big moves.

I then flipped the whole process, and my performance improved dramatically. The reason this works better is because leading stocks, by definition, lead. Some leaders don't even correct much during a down market. That was the case in 1990 with stocks in the healthcare sector. Names such as Amgen (AMGN) and U.S. Surgical (small unknown companies back then) barely undercut their 50-day moving averages during what was a pretty severe bear market. They turned out to be huge winners in the subsequent bull market.

Ryan: It is usually a bottom-up approach, but sometimes I see a group move developing, and I scan the group trying to find the best stock within that group. When I do screens over the weekend, I usually sort them in group order with the strongest group at the top of the list. Your best moves occur when the stock you own is in one of the top 25% of all groups.

Zanger: The latter definitely. I look for strong moves in groups, and then after I hone in on a group, I try to focus on the leaders in that group. This is generally true for me, and yet there have been many stocks that I've owned in groups that are not leaders. I have found some great winners in some obscure groups actually.

Ritchie II: I look for stocks first. Whatever I see, I add to my lists, and that often shows where the strength is in terms of what the overall themes are or what groups are falling in and out of favor.

S2-7: How do you find leading industry groups?

Minervini: I let the best-performing stocks lead me to the best groups. The industry group is made up of stocks, so I focus on the individual stocks. Sometimes there are only a few names in a group that look attractive, and other times there are many. For example, the semiconductor industry is made up of a large number of companies. The key is to spot the leaders in the group as early as possible. This takes an eye that can discern individual stock strength during general market and even group weakness. For instance, if the Nasdaq is below its 200-day line and its 50-day line, it may be worth looking into stocks that are above their own 200- and 50-day lines. When the market turns up, those stocks could be your next market leaders.

Ryan: I go through hundreds of stocks a week looking for leadership. Usually, when a stock makes a good move, then there are others in the group also moving. I also find what groups are leading by looking at *Investor's Business Daily* and MarketSmith. As far as I know, those publications are still using the weightings I developed for ranking groups when I worked for O'Neil & Co.

Zanger: I use the chart program from AIQ Trading Systems, and I have built a large list of prior good-moving stocks and indexes that I've entered into my "Tag List." I scroll through this Tag List, stock by stock, every two to three days to gain a sense of which groups of stocks or industries are working well and which ones aren't.

It's a manual process that has worked well for 25 years. By the way, this list contains about 1,400 stocks, making it very labor intensive to scan. But this is the foundation of what we do: spot the setups and the chart patterns as early as possible.

Ritchie II: I don't search for groups; I search for strong stocks and then see if there are any groups or themes that emerge.

S2-8: Do you trade IPOs (initial public offerings)? How do you define momentum in a name that has little trading history?

Minervini: First, I wait for the IPO to have some trading history. I like to see at least three or four weeks. When trading a recent IPO, your time frames are definitely going to be compressed. There is no long-term trend in just a few weeks, so I focus on the stock chart and its price and volume action. I want to see the same characteristics forming in terms of technical and fundamentals as I would in a name that has a longer trading history. If a sound base develops, I buy as the stock emerges from the consolidation, preferably near its all-time high.

Ryan: Yeah, me too. I like to buy an IPO after it has been trading for at least a couple of weeks. The best IPO is one that comes out in a terrible market when no one cares; it then builds a great base of three months or more, and it's one of the first to break into new high ground when the market starts acting better.

Zanger: Some IPOs trade fast right out of the gate and are generally good for a few days to a week or so, and then they rest or base for anywhere from a few weeks to a few months.

I buy the break of any solid pivot area on an IPO just as I would any momentum stock.

Ritchie II: I trade IPOs but not on their initial day. Like Mark and David, generally I like to see that they have traded for at least a few weeks and ideally months before I consider purchasing them. Once an IPO has established a decent range, I treat it similar to any other situation I may be interested in. Still, I may weigh a newer issue a bit heavier, because by definition it isn't as widely followed or as extensively owned by institutions, so you could be looking at a potentially big winner.

S2-9: Do you treat large caps differently from small caps with your selection criteria; if so, how?

Minervini: Large-cap stocks are going to be more widely followed, so it's more likely you end up in a "crowded trade," especially after the stocks get real hot and everyone is talking about them. As a result, the price action will often be more random, so I tend to let these names undercut lows and create shakeouts before getting in. With larger-cap stocks, I will often try to get on board earlier in the range of a correction. The best time to buy the large-cap names is coming out of a bear market or a deep correction. With small caps, I tend to trade them close to new highs because they're less efficiently priced, so I don't have to "beat the crowd" and try to buy lower.

Ryan: When I look at a larger-cap stock, I assume it will have a slower growth rate than that of a smaller company. It's just a matter of numbers; it's hard to double sales in a company that already has annual sales of a billion dollars compared with that of a company with annual sales of $200 million. There is usually more liquidity in a larger-cap company, and it's easier to move in and out. But you will rarely get a price move as great in a large-cap company versus a small-cap company.

Zanger: I usually never look to own large-cap stocks, as they don't generally have the growth rates that I'm looking for. There have been a few that I've owned and traded—stocks like Apple (AAPL), which has close to 6 billion shares outstanding but still has growth rates at 30%. Most stocks I trade are in the 40 million to 800 million share range, with a few recent movers in the 2 billion share range like Facebook Inc. (FB) or Alibaba (BABA). Alibaba got really hot a month after it went public but later crashed. I still managed to lock in a $25 gain before it crashed though.

Ritchie II: The larger the cap the stock is, the more I discount it, and this is simply for the reason that the odds of inefficient pricing are inverse to the size of the stock. By definition, if a stock is covered by many analysts and watched by thousands of traders, then it has a far less probability of being inefficiently priced and thus yielding a quick alpha move. It doesn't mean the stocks shouldn't be traded or purchased at certain times; but in general, if you're looking for alpha, you should be discounting the larger capitalization.

S2-10: Do you short stocks? If yes, how do you decide to flip to the short side, or do you hold longs and shorts at the same time?

Minervini: I rarely trade long and short at the same time. I'm usually long or in cash. In a bear market, I will trade from the short side, and I may also short stocks if I see a top forming and a bunch of leaders breaking down. If I get a major break in a stock, I will sometimes short a low-volume rally; but I enter as the stock starts selling off again and volume starts to increase on the downside.

Ryan: It is rare when you have a market where you can have both longs and shorts. In a market that is trending in one direction, that's the side you should be leaning toward. Markets moving sideways can be very tough to trade both ways. I have made most of my money on the long side and tend to sit on the sidelines during a bear market.

Zanger: I can't say that I short at the same time I'm long. If the market is strong, why be short? Shorts never pay in a strong market. Overall, I rarely short, as I usually focus on such volatile stocks that the snapbacks can be very sudden and take you out of your position so fast that you don't have time to react quickly enough.

I will say that I've had some very successful shorts in my time. But all of them came from stocks that were breaking their long-term, rising, steep trendlines or rising channels and were missing earnings at the same time.

In fact, eBay (EBAY) in 2004 was a very big winner for me when it failed on earnings and I was short 160,000 shares—the stock plunged $20 in less than 10 minutes after posting earnings. The stock continued to move much lower for the first few days following the company's earnings release, and then I covered to lock in the gains. But short sale winners like that are few and far between.

Ritchie II: I have found shorting to be much more difficult than the long side, and I do it far less frequently and in a different manner. For starters, I don't ever short underlying single stocks outright, mainly because, in principle, I don't believe in trading things that can have theoretical unlimited risk. So if I'm going to short a stock, it will only be through options—and usually using spreads where I can very easily define the risk as well as the reward and weigh what I believe the probabilities to be.

The same generally goes for the market as a whole, as I will sometimes short the market indexes but mostly through options or occasionally futures. My style of shorting is usually following a big break; then I look to short a proverbial "dead cat bounce." I don't want to be shorting anything that is in new high ground, as that is a short-term losing proposition in my view.

S2-11: Do you ever wait to trade a "favorite" on your watch list and hold off trading other stocks as a result, while still waiting for that favorite to trigger a buy?

Minervini: I try not to have favorites. Even though my intuitive feel is pretty good, I have learned not to trust my opinion, because it will eventually be wrong. If you have a strong conviction on a trade, it will be difficult to trust the market and divorce your idea. If I wait for a certain stock that I think will take off while others are breaking out, I could miss a key leader. I want to let the market action guide me, not my opinion. Markets are never wrong, but opinions often are.

Ryan: No. If other stocks, with all the characteristics I look for, are starting to go through buy points, I will buy them. That "favorite" on my watch list might never move again, and I would be sitting with equity that could be deployed in stocks moving higher.

Zanger: I do that often, but one must be careful since a new stock emerging from a base before your "favorite" might very well be the next high flyer. I will typically play the new breakout of this less favored stock, and if it runs hard, it could easily become my new favorite. Then if my old favorite breaks out, I can always reduce my position in the new stock and deploy that cash back into my prior favorite.

Ritchie II: Well, "favorite" is a bit of a tricky word because I try not to have favorites, because it can cloud good judgment. However, if there is a stock that I know I want to buy, I will buy it regardless of how many I've purchased beforehand. If I only want to put on a certain amount of exposure and a stock I want to own hasn't triggered, then I have a choice to make. However, I usually don't hold off from other stocks that meet my criteria, as I believe the market to be smarter than I am; so I will try to buy whichever stock goes first.

SECTION THREE

Position Sizing

S3-1: How many stocks do you normally own; do you believe one should concentrate narrowly or diversify broadly?

Minervini: The bottom line is that you're not going to get huge performance consistently if you're diversified all over the place. If you have a significant edge, diversification does not protect you; it dilutes you. I want to concentrate as much of my money as I can in a position up to 25% of my portfolio. I may not start out at 25%, but that's where I would like to be for my best positions. This number is not just off the top of my head; mathematically speaking, the optimal position size for a 2:1 trader is 25%. You can look up "Optimal f" or the "Kelly formula" to get a better understanding of how to determine this.

Of course, with heavy concentration, you have to stay focused on these trades and move out of them immediately if something goes wrong. But that's how you make huge returns, by concentrating and then managing the downside. By doing this, you'll make big money when you're right.

Ryan: Mark is absolutely correct! To make big gains in the stock market, you have to concentrate. I initiate each position with a 10% weighting: 10 positions in my portfolio. I never want to exceed that number of stocks because it gets too hard to closely follow more than that.

If one of my stocks has a nice move up, builds a new base, and starts moving up again, I will increase the position even more. Where it might now be 13% of my portfolio with appreciation, I may buy another 5–7% and move it to an 18–20% position. You see, I will only add to positions that are moving higher and performing well. Positions only become bigger with appreciation and follow on purchases after new bases are formed. If I don't want to go on to margin, I will decrease or eliminate the underperforming positions in my portfolio.

Zanger: That really depends on the market. Is it a strong bull market? What is the length of the bull market? How broad based is it? In very strong markets that don't have a single massive mover, I could have as many as 22 stocks. In more typical markets with fewer strong movers, I might have 8 to 10 stocks and still other times just 5 to 6 stocks. When the market is very choppy with violent down days and gapping all over the place, I might be 10–15% invested in just two or three stocks; or I might go to none at all if the market is extremely choppy like it was in 2014.

In 2006, I got chewed up badly in a very choppy market even as new highs were seen in the market. New highs are not a guarantee. One key to thriving in this game over time is to avoid taking any positions even if there are a few stocks tempting you with new highs. For me, a market with just a few stocks on the move is not a strong validation to trade.

The overall market must be showing strength with higher highs and a significant portion of those market stocks marching into new highs as well. Many strong bases on the charts, as well as strong expanding earnings on a high number of those stocks, are critical indicators of the overall health of the market and ultimately my portfolio.

Ritchie II: The number of stocks varies quite drastically depending on how healthy I perceive the market to be. In defensive periods, I have no positions; in contrast, when I'm fully margined, I may have as many as 20. This also depends upon where I believe we are in the overall cycle of a bull market, but ideally I'd like to be as concentrated as I can be.

I don't believe diversification is necessarily bad, but it's certainly a catchphrase that is overrated if you want to outperform the market. The only way to consistently outperform is to be concentrated in the names that are outperforming. In fact, I would argue that when it comes to trading, anything you hear as generally accepted wisdom should probably be questioned, and diversification is no different.

For example, being more concentrated in a few names is deemed as more risky, and being spread out all over the place is deemed safe. If you had a choice between being able to own 5 stocks and 50, it might appear that owning 50 would be safer; however, how could someone possibly be as focused on 50 positions as he or she could be on 5?

If you are only watching a few names, you will know the minute something is not acting right and be able to act. In addition, how many names can truly outperform? So by definition, if you're in a larger number of stocks, you're guaranteed to have a larger percentage of underperformers—all things being equal—because only a small percentage of stocks really outperform at any given time.

S3-2: How much of your total equity do you put at risk in a typical trade?

Minervini: Usually between 1.25 and 2.50% of my total equity. For example, if I have a 25% position with a 5% stop, then 1.25% of my total equity would be at risk.

Ryan: At the most, I risk 1% of my total equity on each trade. I divide my equity into 10 positions or a 10% weighting on the initial purchase of a position. If I suffer a maximum loss on a stock of 8%, that actually equates to less than a 1% loss. It most cases, I cut the loss before the 8% limit.

Zanger: I keep my stops fairly tight, so I might be risking 2–3% of the value of that one trade. That is, of course, unless it has a massive gap down on bad news, which has happened numerous times in my career, and I could lose 10–15% in each position or more overnight.

In a typical market, I have a maximum of 10% of my account invested per trade; so that means I'm risking just a fraction of 1% (20–30 basis points) of my total equity per trade. On rare occasions, if a stock has massive earnings and spectacular volume on its breakout, then I might stretch my position size up to 25%.

Ritchie II: My risk per trade has gone down on average over the last few years; but on average, a starting position will get about 50 basis points of risk, and then I will scale up from there.

S3-3: What number of positions will generally get you to fully invested?

Minervini: Rarely more than 10 to 12 positions, but I like to get as much money as I can in 4 to 8 of the best names.

Ryan: In my portfolio it would be 10 or less. I divide my portfolio into 10 different segments, starting with an initial purchase of 5%. If it quickly starts to work, then the position is increased to 10%. From there, the movement of the stock will determine how big the position will get within the portfolio. If the stock makes a nice gain and is now 15% of the portfolio and builds a new base, I might increase the position as it breaks out, and it is now 20% of the portfolio.

Zanger: That depends on the market and how many great moving stocks and sectors there are. It could be anywhere from 8 to 25 stocks depending on market conditions.

Ritchie II: Anywhere from 4 to 12 generally, which has more to do with the confidence I have in my trading of late as well as where I think we are in the intermediate-term cycle—i.e., beginning, middle, later stage of a bull run, etc.

S3-4: What is the maximum-size position you would trade? Do you ever put your entire account in one stock?

Minervini: My maximum is the optimal 25%. If you're more conservative or new at trading, maybe you can have 10–12% positions (8–10 stocks). But there is no need to own 25 names, and you should never risk your entire portfolio in just one name; that's way too risky!

I learned this lesson on a near miss in the early 1990s. I was thinking of buying a stock—I think it was called Future Healthcare of America—but I didn't. The next morning the stock gapped down 80%. Right then I realized I can never risk it all in just one name. But if I have a 25% position, I have enough concentration to make really big gains; however, if something catastrophic happens, the loss is still recoverable.

Ryan: When the overall market is acting well and most of my stocks are moving higher, I can get a position to a 25% weighting, but that is only after appreciation of the stock has caused the weighting to get bigger. I won't start a position at 25% weighting.

Zanger: I have been "all in" just once, and it nearly wiped me out completely. The stock of a certain company was trading at $27 on Friday and went down to $6 on Monday after *Barron's* ran a story that my stock was a total fraud based on the company's accounting practices. Thank God that stock was not marginable, or I would have had to hand all my belongings to a bankruptcy judge.

On the other side, I once had a very large position in Google Inc. (GOOG) around the time it first started to run in 2005. It amounted to about 50% of my account at the time. That was a major success for me and also was the last time

I loaded up so large on a single stock. Apple Inc. (AAPL) in 2012 made two big runs, and I was in at no more than a 30% weighting each time it ran.

As a general rule, if it's a very powerful mover coming out from a great base with spectacular earnings, I would buy up to 20% in one stock.

Ritchie II: I normally don't go over 25% in one stock, but there have been a few select situations where I've gone as big as 50% in one name. I wouldn't advocate putting all your account in one stock, and I have never done that. I would only have a large position in a name that I already have a profit in, so that I build into a larger position as the trade is working for me.

S3-5: What is the minimum position size you normally trade as a percentage of your account equity?

Minervini: If things are not working out and stops are being hit repeatedly, I progressively scale back my position sizing. So there is no minimum under that scenario. However, I generally like to have at least a 5% position to start.

Ryan: When the market is not in a solid uptrend, I start my positions smaller at 5% and then work them higher as they succeed.

Zanger: Well, if it's a tough, choppy environment, I might do 1% just to stay in tune with the market. I think keeping a hand in the market helps you maintain a better sense of when things start to improve. With no skin in the game, it's too easy to be on the beach or golf course when things pivot, and then you miss the moves.

Ritchie II: I don't have a minimum specified amount, because sometimes there may be a thinner name that I can't buy very much of, but I'll still take a position based upon what I believe to be appropriate in terms of liquidity. For names where liquidity isn't an issue (which is most names), I generally don't take smaller than a 6.25% position.

S3-6: Do you position-size each trade based on the amount of dollars at risk or a fixed percentage?

Minervini: Sometimes I go into a trade and say to myself, "I'm only willing to risk a certain dollar amount on this trade," and then I back into that number. But most of the time, I use a percentage. Generally my "toe-in-the-water" trades are 5–10% positions. And when things are working well, I trade wide open with 25% of my portfolio in a few of the best names.

Ryan: I work on a fixed percentage. As the account gets larger, the percentages stay the same.

Zanger: I approach each new trade by calculating how much I stand to lose if the stock gaps down tomorrow. I want damage control in place before entering the trade, not after. If I'm comfortable with that potential dollar loss, I size up the stock's liquidity, which directly determines how quickly I can get out should the stock swoon on me. Then and only then, will I move forward to the final important factors. If it's a top-notch company with a strong global presence and great earnings, I might then put up to 20% of my portfolio in that single stock.

More typically, in a strong broad-based market move, 5–7% is a better average for each stock, but I will put more in the most powerful movers. You have to have a good feel for the markets to determine your best position sizing. That instinct really only comes with having been through the washing machine a few times to empty the spare change out of your pockets and leave you clean.

Ritchie II: I determine the number of shares based upon a percentage of the capital I am allocating to equities, but I have a very good idea of what my average loss is over time, so I always have the amount of equity that I'm risking in mind both on an individual trade and across the overall portfolio. If there is no need for liquidity provision, then I generally trade in fractions of my largest position; so, for example, if 25% is my largest line, I will trade in 12.5% or 6.25% increments.

S3-7: Do you increase your position size based on the growth of your account throughout the year; or do you use the same position size the whole year to maintain the same dollar risk per trade?

Minervini: I use the whole account. But I would recommend that a new trader hold off a bit until the account is up maybe 25% or even 50% before increasing.

Ryan: The size of a position is determined by a percentage of the entire account. It doesn't matter if it is $100,000 or $1 million; a starting position is 10% of the whole account.

Zanger: Good question and one I've had to deal with for years. I try not to increase the size of my trades as the year goes on. This is predicated on the presumption that the market is advancing while my account is progressing, which increases the probability that the market is becoming more extended. As a result, it's vulnerable to a correction, which can become more costly to me from the increased risk related to my larger position sizes.

Ritchie II: I think of this in terms of my risk of drawdowns, so as to be aggressive enough where I can increase my position size upon success, but defensive enough so that I don't have to cut sizes every time I hit a bad period. The way I do this is by looking at my past trading to determine what my normal percentage drawdowns are. Once I have that level established, I don't increase my position size until I have earned a significantly larger portion than my average drawdown.

S3-8: What gives you the confidence to take a very large position?

Minervini: The lower the risk, the larger the position I feel comfortable taking. Risk is defined by how big my stop loss is and how liquid the name is. I grade the trade in terms of a poker hand. Aces and kings get my fullest attention—those are premium hands—while a pair of sevens may only get a partial weighting. I also want to have a string of successful trades backlogged so I'm pyramiding larger risk on the heels of my gains.

Ryan: It first starts with the company having all the character-istics I look for in a great winning stock. Second, if the stock is in a strong uptrend with little selling when it corrects, that gives me the most confidence. Finally, if we are in a bull mar-ket, that helps all stocks achieve higher prices and would give me added confidence to take larger positions.

Zanger: Having years of trading helps. Identifying aggres-sive stocks with great volume characteristics and tremendous earnings can't be beat. But being able to recognize even the most subtle bullish and bearish chart patterns is a big leg up that helps my confidence every time.

Even a powerful runner breaking out can get into trouble early and flash a bearish chart pattern that gives a heads-up. I might reduce 30–50% of that stock position right away or get out completely based on something subtle in that chart's behavior.

If I sell out half my position after a $20 move up, I've locked in a $20 gain. If the stock continues up, I'm still mak-ing good gains on the remaining 50% of that position. If the stock caves, I've locked in a $20 gain on 50% of my orig-inal investment. Nothing helps your confidence better than win-win scenarios like this when you have a perceived edge in reading the charts.

Ritchie II: Success. This is a concept that Mark Minervini has pounded into the heads of his followers, and I've been fortu-nate to grasp it early in my career. It's always much easier to trade larger on the heels of success, at least for me. And that reduces the risk of ruin going forward. In addition, the combination of having done my homework and being prepared takes out the emotion from trading larger.

S3-9: How do you determine the "quality" of a setup? If one stock is more deserving of capital versus another, how do you quantify that? Or do you keep all position sizes equal?

Minervini: I try to keep them equal, but it doesn't always work out that way for several reasons. First is liquidity and volatility; if the stock is really small or too volatile, I'm not going take big risk. The other is my trading rhythm; if I have not experienced some successful trades, I'm usually trading smaller, even in names that look deserving. The "quality" of a setup is determined by price and volume action and earnings power. The better names have stronger price performance and the strongest earnings and sales.

Ryan: After scanning probably millions of charts over my 40 years of investing, there is a certain look that a great stock will have before it begins its move. It is usually the symmetry of the price action and the tight trading range of the stock in the last week or two before a stock breaks out that, together, give me the confidence to buy a full position quickly. The stock also has to have strong fundamentals to go along with the price action to give me the confidence that this could be a big winner.

Zanger: Volatility is a primary factor along with a solid base. How long the base is and whether it's a very high-level extended base or a first- or second-stage base are strong secondary considerations. Stocks that can make large intraday moves are stocks that qualify for my money. The bigger the potential move from that solid base, the more money I want to devote to that trade. More than likely, the stock has given me plenty of signals that a big move is coming.

Ritchie II: I certainly don't keep all position sizes equal, and in principle I believe you should have the most capital in the ideas you have the most conviction in, regardless of asset class or strategy. Quantifying the quality of a setup is truly an art and one I'm trying to get better at all the time.

Generally I look at technicals first, then fundamentals, and then the group. The best situations have all three; however, that doesn't necessarily mean I will take the largest position. That also depends heavily upon my recent trading results, my overall exposure, and liquidity, as sometimes a really good situation may be a very small-cap situation, where I can't have a huge position. But I'll put on as much as I'm comfortable, because above all else, I still want to be able to get out of a situation very quickly if I need to.

SECTION FOUR

Technical Analysis

S4-1: How do you go beyond being interested in a name to actually buying it? What specifically do you look for with regard to price and volume before buying a stock?

Minervini: A volatility contraction in price accompanied by a dry-up in volume or a selling vacuum. To make big money fast with momentum stocks, you must learn how to position yourself in the strongest part of the move and time the trade correctly. After you spot a stock in a strong trend, the volatility contraction pattern or VCP, is the best way to determine if a stock has carved out a line of least resistance with the potential to blast off through a pivot point. For a detailed explanation of this setup and how to trade it, you could refer to the chapter "A Picture Is Worth a Million Dollars" in my book *Trade Like a Stock Market Wizard: How to Achieve Superperformance in Stocks in Any Market* (McGraw-Hill, 2013).

Ryan: I look for very stable price action. Like Mark, I don't like volatility in the price movement before I buy. There should be a period of a week or more of very quiet and very tight price action before a stock makes a move. That stability usually occurs after a larger base has formed and is in the upper half of its chart pattern.

Zanger: In the simplest terms possible, it's all about price action during the day. A lack of standout behavior in a stock's price behavior is a clue that the stock is an underperformer. To use an analogy from the horse racing world, I'm looking for thoroughbreds like Secretariat, Affirmed, or American Pharoah, and they come along rarely. So you very much need to stay in tune with the market every day to hone your skills for picking out these massive movers and learn to catch them early.

Ritchie II: The general rule of thumb for me is that I want to see a stock that has acted in an orderly manner where it is in an uptrend followed by a consolidation period. Ideally it won't have a good deal of volume in the consolidation period, and ideally if volume is below average, then that is even better. Actually pulling the trigger is just a matter of deciding which names I know I want to purchase when they reach certain price points; others I may want to watch a bit first. But as a general rule, I have these decisions made before the day starts.

If the action during the day is really good, I may be more apt to put on more risk and buy more positions if current ones are acting well, and conversely then I let the price action dictate whether the initial day's plan should be more aggressive or conservative.

S4-2: Would you invest in a stock with unfavorable fundamentals in a very bullish environment if technical price action is good?

Minervini: Many of the best trades occur when you have fundamentals, technicals, and a bullish general market all in your favor. So I try to focus on companies that have solid fundamental and technical characteristics during a healthy market environment. However, life is not perfect. Stocks that set up well technically, in a manner I refer to as "unexplained strength," are often good risk-reward plays because they are less obvious and not as likely to be "crowded." So, yes, I will trade stocks with a lack of apparent fundamentals when the chart is really strong.

Most of the time when I ignore surface fundamentals, the stock is in a very high-momentum situation, and the chart is saying that something really big is definitely going on. This can occur in biotech and medical stocks that often trade on the promise of a new drug or the approval of the FDA (U.S. Food and Drug Administration).

Ryan: I might buy solely on the technicals, but that would be just for a trade, and I don't do that too often. I want both the fundamentals and the technical aspects of a stock to be going in the same direction. If both are present, it could power a stock for a nice long move for months and even years. If the technicals are only present, the earnings better start coming in soon because the move is not going to last long. I don't day-trade, and I like to manage a position as long as the stock is in an uptrend. If you have a very short-term time frame, then maybe you can go with just a technical setup.

Zanger: You bet I would! As Mark pointed out, some of the best growth stocks move up well in advance of good earnings coming out. First Solar Inc. (FSLR) went public in late 2006 at around $24 a share and had no earnings, and yet the stock ran hard all the way up to $300 per share in just 18 months before solid earnings came out.

By the way, those earnings back then were incredible, and they proved to be the top of that stock's move at just over $300 a share; and since then, the stock has come down to $40 in 2015. A stock's movement often precedes good earnings, though that is not always the case, especially in the late stages of a bull market.

Ritchie II: I buy under both conditions. I like to have the fundamentals, but if the chart looks really good, I'll buy it even with poor fundamentals. To Dave's point, most of my stocks are trades, not long-term investments.

S4-3: Would a stock with poor fundamentals but excellent relative strength trading near a new 52-week high still qualify as a leader? One could argue that there had to be some fundamental reason for the high RS.

Minervini: Well, it would qualify as a price leader, which by definition makes it a market leader because it's been outperforming the market. A market leader can be measured in terms of price action, earnings, sales, etc. I prefer to have all of the above, but as I said earlier, life isn't perfect.

The textbook definition of a market leader is price action versus the market and its industry group peers. Sometimes you have the earnings on the table, and sometimes you don't. However, history shows that 70% of big market movers have earnings on the table *before* they make a big move. If you're trading biotech stocks, however, more often than not, earnings are not on the table.

Ryan: Yes, you can say it is a leader based on price. However, the more reliable leaders are those that have both strong price strength and good earnings.

Zanger: It sure could qualify. As Mark Minervini just pointed out, this is the case with most biotech stocks, as many of them are making tremendous moves with no earnings at all. They are trading on future earnings of new drugs or compounds they have discovered.

Many stocks can break out and run up prior to strong earnings coming out. As has been noted for a hundred years or more, the market moves up six to nine months in advance of good economic news, and stocks pretty much do the same.

Ritchie II: Absolutely, if a stock is "leading" in terms of relative strength, then it's a leader and it's on my list as a potential buy.

S4-4: I assume you require stocks you buy to be in a price uptrend. How do you define an uptrend?

Minervini: Did you ever show up as the first one at a party? I bet you sat around for a while waiting for things to really get going; the party probably didn't pick up until after everyone was there. It's the same with trading. I never want to try to be the first one to the party in a stock trade. Why? I want to see some interest in the stock, preferably from big institutional investors. Before I join the "party," I want to make sure there's a party going on to join!

Specifically, I never go long a stock that is trading below its declining 200-day moving average (assuming 200 days of trading exist). No matter how attractive the fundamentals look, I won't consider buying a stock that is in a long-term downtrend, because going long stocks in long-term downtrends significantly lowers your odds of owning a big winner. If you want to increase your chances, you should focus on stocks that are in price uptrends. Momentum stocks by definition are in strong price trends.

Ryan: About 90% of the stocks I buy are in strong uptrends. I define an uptrend as a stock with its 50-day moving average above its 200-day moving average and both are trending higher. Even stronger uptrends can be defined as the 20-day moving average above the 50-day, and the 50-day is above the 200-day moving average. I tend to concentrate on those stocks that are in strong uptrends with an IBD relative strength greater than 80.

Occasionally I buy a stock that is a turnaround situation. But I only buy that turnaround as the stock's downtrend is over; the price has gone sideways for at least three to six months and starts to turn up. A recent example is Lululemon Athletica Inc. (LULU) as it turned up in early December 2014. In six weeks, it was up 40%. At the time of my purchase, the stock was trading above the 50-day and the 200-day moving averages. The 50-day moving average was in an in an uptrend, and the 200-day had flattened.

Zanger: Uptrends are my best friend and certainly my preference, but I have bought stocks coming up from inverted head-and-shoulders patterns, which happens after a stock has finished a series of lower lows and lower highs. Uptrending stocks to me are stocks that are stairstepping higher with a series of higher highs and higher lows with solid tight bases in between these steps.

Ritchie II: Yes, I never break this rule. If a stock is not in a long-term uptrend where it's trading above its 200, 150, or 50-day moving average, I won't consider it.

S4-5: Do you use any indicators such as stochastics or MACD (moving average convergence-divergence) or ATR (average true range)?

Minervini: None. Just price, volume, and a few moving averages for smoothing and company fundamentals, mainly earnings, sales, and margins. But what's important is that you use what works for you. If using stochastics works for you or if trading by the way the stars align in the sky works, great! Make it yours, and be the best you can at it. There's certainly more than one way to skin the cat.

Ryan: I do look at stochastics and MACD. They add additional information about the strength of a move; but I rely mostly on the price and volume action combined with the fundamental aspects of the company. I don't want to complicate the issue. You can start looking at so many indicators that you get yourself confused. Keep it simple.

Zanger: I use the AIQ Trading Expert's SK-SD more than any other. Since I've used it for 24 years, I'm very comfortable with it, and it's much more reliable for me than MACD. I never used ATR, so I couldn't comment on that.

Ritchie II: I find the ATR measurement to be quite helpful in short-term futures trading, but I use it on a fairly short time frame, because I want to know what is the normal volatility level that the market has been trading within during the last few sessions and specifically whether that level is advancing quickly. I want to know what kind of noise is normal in a market in hopes of placing my stops outside that level, and ATR is what I tend to use. I don't have any experience using MACD or stochastic indicators.

S4-6: What are the most important technical considerations to buy a stock?

Minervini: The price and volume action as well as the relative strength of the stock versus the market and versus other stocks in the same group. Ultimately, the verdict of the market is all that matters. Even if the fundamentals are strong, I'm not going to buy a stock unless the price and volume action is constructive.

Ryan: The price pattern and volume of a stock are my most important indicators. They are the first things I look at, and they carry the greatest weight when I make my buy and sell decisions. The relationship between price and volume gives me the best indication of the future price direction.

Zanger: The most important indicator is the overall market trending up with higher highs and higher lows, and the same goes for the stocks that I look to buy. Next would be a well-defined base and then the strength of the group.

Ritchie II: I don't use many technical "indicators," just mainly price and volume, although the next best thing is the stock's relative strength rating.

S4-7: Do you prefer to buy momentum names on pullbacks or on breakouts?

Minervini: Most of my pullback buys are entered while the stock is still in a base, before a breakout even occurs. Sometimes I buy on a pullback to a previous breakout level, and more rarely I buy on a pullback to a moving average like the 50-day after a breakout, but I'm hoping to already be in the stock before that occurs.

I buy whenever there are good low-risk setups—breakouts or pullback buys—whatever is working. I try to find the cycle's technical "theme" and then play the market's tendencies within that theme. The key is to make quality decisions on each trade. You don't want to take too much risk, whether it's a pullback trade or a breakout.

Ryan: It really depends on the type of market you are in. If it is a choppy market, breakouts have a tendency to fail or not make much progress. In that case, I buy more pullbacks. In a strong uptrending market, breakouts tend to keep going, and if you wait for a pullback, you could miss a big move.

Zanger: Breakouts are best, and the larger gains are to be had there, of course. But if I miss the original breakout, then I will have no choice but to buy a pullback to get in. This is where the 10-day moving average comes in, or alternatively, using short-term time frames such as 5-minute charts or 30-minute charts.

Ritchie II: I prefer breakouts because the best situations don't often pull back much, so I would much rather pay up and buy a breakout. That doesn't mean I won't buy a pullback, but generally I will only buy a pullback after a stock has success-fully broken out and has then pulled back in an orderly way, often several days to even a few weeks later.

S4-8: How do you define a breakout?

Minervini: Well, a technical breakout is when a stock trades above a predetermined price level, usually coming out of a base or consolidation. If you're using the previous day's high as a buy point, the stock trading above that level would con-stitute a breakout, so it really depends on what strategy you are using and what line in the sand you consider important.

Ryan: A breakout is a stock emerging out of a base or side-ways consolidation. I like a base to be at least four weeks or longer. As the stock breaks out, the volume should be larger than average. The volume should increase at least 25% or more. The best moves start with very big increases in volume of 100% or more.

Zanger: It's when a stock hits the pivot area of the base and explodes out from it on massive volume and never looks back at the pivot area. It might run for two or three days and then rest a week or so and then accelerate higher on sizable volume again. Stocks that vacillate at the breakout area tend to be prone to failure or have weak upside potential.

Ritchie II: The word *breakout* is a generic term that refers to price moving above something. It can be a breakout above a trendline, an old high, or some other kind of pivot. Ideally I'd like to have price breakouts occur for all three examples above; however, at a minimum would be the stock breaking above some kind of pivot. Additionally, stocks can have fundamental breakouts as well, for example, a breakout of earnings and sales.

S4-9: I've been involved in many false breakouts only to have the stock return to within the base and consolidate much longer. Would you say that adding 10–20 cents to the buy point would be an effective technique to avoid getting sucked into false breakouts?

Minervini: I don't usually buy just a penny above the buy point. I will generally wait for the stock to trade 5, 10, or even 20 cents above the pivot level. The only time I go in guns blazing is when things are working really well and I'm holding profitable trades. Then I may loosen up a bit and give stocks the benefit of the doubt. Otherwise, I usually wait and would rather pay a little higher price to make sure the stock is advancing. But even then, the stock could turn back down. There really is no magic number.

With that said, if I buy a stock and it falls back and consolidates longer, I will usually stay with the name as long as it doesn't stop me out or something more attractive doesn't turn up. Keep in mind, you don't have to buy everything at one price. I usually scale in and add as the position starts working. This is the subtle art of executing your trades.

Ryan: No, I would stick with the exact price you determined for the stock to break out. If recent breakouts haven't been successful, then you might want to start with a smaller position and then add quickly if the stock closes well and continues higher the next day. You don't have to do all your buying on one day, but adjust the size of your position based on the strength of the stock and the market.

Zanger: If the market is choppy and not many stocks are getting solid breakouts, then yes, I would raise the bar and not buy very many shares, as I might have to check out just as fast as I got in.

Ritchie II: In my opinion there is no technique that will allow you to avoid false breakouts; that is the main inherent risk in trading breakouts—they often fail. Raising the trigger area a bit isn't always a bad idea; however, I think it is very stock specific.

For example, I am much more apt to wait until the price is firmly breaking out in a more liquid name because previous highs or lows tend to be more obvious technical points and are more prone to be shaken out or run through by other participants, market makers, etc.

This is why a breakout trader should always be willing to "pay up" to a degree, because the best trades by definition won't be losers even if you have to pay up to get in them. They will still get away from you with relative ease if they are truly legitimately breaking out, and it is ultimately the breakout trader's job to use whatever tools and techniques possible to sift out the stocks that aren't really breaking out in earnest.

S4-10: Do you ever build a position during a low-volume consolidation or sideways movement, or do you always wait for the stock to break out?

Minervini: I generally wait for the stock to break out or at the very least start turning up through a pivot point. I don't want to sit with dead money, so even if I try to get in before the breakout, I always require the stock to be moving in the direction of the trade. If you're playing for a decent move, you don't gain much of an advantage getting in a few pennies or even 10 cents early. So what's the point?

Ryan: I wait for the stock to break out of a sideways movement. If you buy when the stock is still in a base, you run the risk that the stock will actually break to the downside. I think it's better to wait until a stock breaks out. If you buy early, you don't know if it will actually break out to the upside. It could have some bad news, or the market could turn down, and you are then sitting with a loss.

Zanger: I'll wait for the breakout 90% of the time. Once volume dries up and the stock appears to be consolidating, you just never know when it might get hit by a downgrade and drop $10–$20; or it lowers earnings guidance, and the stock can drop like a swatted fly and never rebound. It's always best to wait until "judgment day" when the breakout tells you definitively that there's plenty of gas in the tank—or that the tank is empty. Why have your money sitting in a stock that is going nowhere? Save yourself a lot of guessing and buy a stock that is actually breaking out.

Ritchie II: If I'm going to add to an existing position, it's only when the consolidation or sideways action is resolving itself. Again, I want to see the price action to be confirming; so I'd rather buy more as it's breaking out of the consolidation period. This to me is really a function of personality, as both are viable approaches. I often buy a little on the way up while the stock is still in its consolidation period before it officially triggers a breakout to new relative highs, at which point I may add more.

S4-11: How do you assess a stock that is consistently making new highs on lower volume?

Minervini: Poor demand. But I wouldn't sell a stock just because it's going up on low volume. Stocks can sometimes go quite a distance on anemic volume.

Ryan: In general, you want a stock to rise on higher volume and pull back on lower volume because the buying and selling by institutions is what moves stocks in the market, and the institutions can't hide the fact that they have to buy in size.

The most important area to concentrate on is what volume is doing at key points like breakouts to new highs, breakdowns from bases, and even when a stock undercuts a previous low.

When a stock is breaking out of a base, I like to see huge volume that is many times greater than the average volume during the last 50 days. I also like to see that the volume continues higher for at least three days. That will be a sign that the large institutions and hedge funds are also buying. If the stock breaks to new highs on volume for one day and has no follow-through, then that indicates to me it was just a bunch of traders playing the new high.

Once the stock has had a nice breakout for a number of days, then the volume can go back to average daily volume or even less than average. It's like a rocket blasting off; you need lots of fuel to get it off the launchpad, but once it's in orbit, it doesn't need nearly as much volume to keep it going higher.

Zanger: Many of the best-moving stocks of all time break out on massive volume, and the move up could take three to four months before buyers start to dry up. Making new highs on lower volume is a natural part of a stock's move. In such a case, most of the stock will have been taken off the market by folks with early knowledge.

The people who show up late to the party buy what little stock is left, but by this time, which is usually anywhere from three to eight months into the stock's run, those early buyers are ready to lock in their gains. Selling comes quickly at this stage, and those late to the party get burned as those early institutional buyers start to sell.

Ritchie II: I like to look at volume in connection with the price action. For example, if a stock breaks out on huge volume but only closes up marginally higher, that tells me there was almost an equal number of buyers and sellers at those newly high prices, which means the breakout is probably suspect. A stock making higher highs on low volume isn't bad; after all, price is king for me, although I may be less apt to hold a situation like that for a big move if I feel the volume isn't there.

S4-12: If a stock opens within the prior day's range and advances beyond your buy point, but it shows average or even lower-than-average volume at the end of the day, would that be a signal for caution?

Minervini: Not necessarily. I wouldn't sell a stock just because it broke out on low volume. Sometimes the volume comes in the next day or several days later. In that case, I would like to see the stock follow through on higher volume. On the other hand, if the breakout was on low volume and then the stock sold off on high volume, that would usually get me to sell or at least reduce my position.

Ryan: I might wait for the close to see what kind of volume has traded to make my decision. Optimally, I want to see volume; the bigger the volume and the longer it lasts, the better it is.

Zanger: Volume is what makes the stocks move; so, yes, if it had lighter-than-normal volume on a breakout day, I would pass.

Ritchie II: No, if the stock goes beyond my buy point and shows very little price follow-through or volume, then there's no reason to do anything other than sit on my hands. At this point, the price action is sort of agnostic; it's not confirming nor denying anything, and markets often act this way.

S4-13: How do you evaluate volume if a stock starts moving early in the day and there isn't much volume information yet?

Minervini: Intraday I extrapolate the volume. If it's 10:30 a.m. and a stock that trades 500,000 shares per day has already traded 175,000, that's the equivalent of the stock trading around 1 million total shares for the day. In that scenario, I would buy. Then I would check the end-of-the-day tally to see if the volume remained strong and continued to keep pace with the level when the stock started moving.

Ryan: If the base is perfect, I might start with a small position and see if the volume picks up by the close of the trading day. I want to see large volume because that is a sign that mutual funds and hedge funds are also buying. Too many stocks these days have one-day breakouts on light volume and then fall back into the base.

Zanger: I have a tool that runs a ratio of the stock's volume history, and if my ratio is way above normal, then I start to move in. The greater the ratio, the more confident I am about moving into the stock. By the end of the day, volume should be 50% or more above its recent history, or my trade would become suspect. eSignal can provide you with my ratio tool known as the Zanger Volume Ratio (ZVR) on most updated eSignal programs.

Ritchie II: There is no exact science to intraday volume. You can do some basic math to extrapolate a good estimate; for example, if it has traded 50% of its average daily volume in the first hour, you can make a good assumption that the stock is going to have a well-above-average-volume day. However, you never know how constant the volume flow is going to be, and it's always highest at the opening and closing of the day. The more important thing early in a day is to see if the stock is being bought in earnest—such as if it breaks out early, you want to see offers being gobbled up, which shows that someone is taking all the available supply.

S4-14: Would you buy a stock even if there isn't large volume accompanying the breakout or pivot and hope the volume comes in later?

Minervini: Well, intraday you don't always know if the final volume tally is going to meet a minimum requirement if the stock starts to move early in the day. You can extrapolate, but even with that, the volume could be light in the morning and pick up later in the day after you're already in. I usually buy the stock on price action and then look for confirming volume. I can always sell it if things don't progress favorably.

Ryan: Again, if the fundamentals are very good and the base is just right, I will buy a smaller position and then add to it if the volume and the price continue to rise.

Zanger: Volume must be rushing in when I'm buying, and the stock must finish the day with a large percentage increase in volume, or I'm out. It's that simple. There is no way to buy or sell a large number of shares on minimal volume.

Ritchie II: Absolutely, especially if you are early, there often won't be large-volume buying, so I'm happy to let the trade play out and see if volume is supportive in coming days.

S4-15: Why would you buy a stock without having volume confirmation (determined at the close), rather than wait until volume comes into the stock and buy it then?

Minervini: Because I could miss the move. Many stocks start off slowly and then pick up pace after they have already moved up.

Ryan: Yes, Mark is correct. What can happen is the volume is very light as the stock is going through the buy point, and then the volume comes in later in the day or even the next day, and by that time it might be too extended. So I would buy, but it would be a smaller position, and not add until the volume came into the stock.

Zanger: When volume starts to surge early in the day and the stock crosses the buy area, I'm in. By the end of the day, volumes should confirm. If you wait until volume has confirmed at the end of the day for your entry, the stock might be up $10 and far past the buy area.

Ritchie II: Yes, I don't ever wait for volume confirmation. I like to see it after the fact, of course, and confirmation may lead me to add, but I don't wait for it initially.

S4-16: If volume does not continue to come in and move the stock higher after *X* number of days after you bought it, would you consider selling the position (i.e., a time stop)?

Minervini: If it's going up and I'm at a decent profit, I would probably stay with it even if the volume is low. But I would watch it closely and be likely to sell it more quickly should the stock start to reverse.

Ryan: If the stock is at a profit and the stock hasn't shown the kind of volume I was looking for, I would move my stop up to the breakeven point and give the stock more time.

Zanger: The first two days out of the base are the most important in regard to volume and price behavior. After that period, holding would depend on the depth of the volume dry-up followed by the price behavior when volume recedes. I have nothing preset in my mind like a time stop, since I only respond to volume and price behavior independent of time after those first two days.

Ritchie II: I view price as king, so even if volume hasn't come into the stock but the price is holding up or moving higher, then I will stick with the trade.

S4-17: Do you have any volume rules that you require on a breakout day, such as volume greater than *X* number of days' average, or does it have to be greater by *X* percent?

Minervini: I like to see the volume eclipse its own 50-day average. Some use a 50% increase above the 50-day average; the more volume, the better.

Ryan: Yes, the bigger, the better. I like to see the volume up at least 25%, but 100–200% increases in volume show me that large institutions are also actively buying the stock.

Zanger: A good rule of thumb is to look for a volume surge by the end of the day that is greater than 50% of the stock's 20-day or 30-day average. I currently use the 20-day average myself.

Ritchie II: I don't have hard rules; but ideally I would like to see above-average volume.

S4-18: How patient are you with pullbacks shortly after the breakout to or just below the breakout area?

Minervini: It is common for a stock to pull back to the breakout area and even undercut it; this will happen about half the time even in some of the best names. Of course, I would prefer that the stock follows through for several days to get me at a profit right away; the strongest stocks out of the gate will often turn out to be the biggest winners. However, as long as the stock holds my initial stop, I usually stay with the trade. I often move my stop to my breakeven point once the stock moves up a decent amount. Until then, I wait for the trade to prove me right or wrong.

Ryan: If the stock didn't pull back on huge volume retreating into the base, I will give it up to a 5–8% loss. I never like it when a stock breaks out and quickly falls back into the base. That is not a sign of a strong stock. I want breakouts on strong volume that continue for at least three consecutive days. That is the sign of big institutional buying.

Zanger: I sell it. That's exactly how I handle that situation. A winning race horse never backs into the starting gate after the gate has opened. Neither should a great winning stock.

Ritchie II: A pullback to the breakout area is pretty normal, so I don't cut things out so long as they haven't taken out stop levels; breakout levels are often revisited, and I consider that normal action.

S4-19: How many trade setups or chart patterns do you typically trade?

Minervini: Maybe six or eight. But most are just permutations of my basic breakout and pullback buy techniques. The main thing I look for is VCP characteristics; that's a contraction in volatility from left to right during the consolidation phase.

Ryan: I basically simplify it down to two, breakouts and pull-backs. Don't get confused by all the different formations. You don't really have to look for cup with handles, or saucers, or "W" formations. You just have to draw a line across the top of where most of the stock's trading has taken place. Then you buy as it moves through that line. It is as simple as that. I always like to see a very tight price pattern before the stock breaks to new highs. Buying pullbacks are a bit more complicated but offer another entry point to get aboard a leading stock.

Zanger: Well, I can't say I've counted them all but somewhere in the neighborhood of eight or so. Mostly flat channels or bull flags with a few cup-and-handle patterns every now and then. Descending channels work too, but usually there are frequent shakeouts going on when they break to the upside before they really get going.

Ritchie II: I trade probably four to five different variations on the same overall theme, that being stocks in long-term uptrends coming out of consolidation periods. The variations themselves may be in how long the stock has consolidated, what the different pivot- or resistance-point formations are, how volume is acting, how close the stock is to new highs, etc.

SECTION FIVE

Fundamentals

S5-1: Do you find stocks with proper fundamentals and then look at the charts or vice versa?

Minervini: I look at the chart and the long-term trend first, because I'm not going to buy a stock even if it has good fundamentals if the chart is bad and the stock is in a downtrend.

Ryan: I rely heavily on the chart of a company. I usually go through hundreds if not thousands of charts every week looking for a proper setup. If I see what I'm looking for on the chart, then I look to the fundamentals to see if they are strong. I want both the fundamentals and the technical characteristics of the stock to be in an uptrend. I have much more confidence in holding a stock that has good fundamentals than if I'm buying based solely on a good chart. There are so many stocks to choose from, why not go with the one that has the best characteristics. If I hear of a company with great fundamentals, I always check to see if the chart confirms what I'm hearing.

Zanger: I look at the charts first since chart patterns have led me to my biggest winners. If a stock has great fundamentals, more than likely it has really good earnings and revenue growth. It simply follows that at some point this stock will have a really great-looking chart pattern that grew from those strong fundamentals.

Ritchie II: I always look at charts first, because if the stock doesn't meet some basic technical criteria first, then I won't even consider purchasing it regardless of the fundamentals.

S5-2: Before you buy, how much time do you typically put into researching a stock (fundamentals, news stories, chart, etc.)?

Minervini: If it's a name that I'm not already familiar with, I will put in as much time as I need to investigate the earnings, recent news stories, and other companies in the same industry group. However, many stocks are names I already know and have been following, so it's just a matter of watching when the technical picture develops into an entry point and monitoring earnings reports along the way.

Ryan: Because I take a big-picture view of the fundamentals and don't get caught up in the minute details of each earnings report, it could be a matter of minutes for me to make a decision. But I am usually more successful if I spend a number of hours researching the fundamentals, listening to conference calls, investigating the company's website to really get to know where the company has been and its future plans.

Zanger: Not much time at all, to tell you the truth. I used to do lots of fundamental work, but I found myself wanting to believe in that stock since I had done so much work on it. All it took was two spectacular blowups that nearly wiped me out in the mid-1990s, and from that point forward I gave that up.

Now it's all about price behavior of stocks, and I let the market tell me which stock to own and which stock to avoid. That constitutes 80% of my research. The other 20% is reviewing earnings on the best-moving stocks in the market. I usually find they do, in fact, have very strong earnings and revenues to support the price behavior that caught my eye.

Ritchie II: This depends upon how good I consider the technicals to be. I will always do some preliminary research into the company, such as what it does, what sector it is in, and what its earnings and sales are, but it isn't always extensive.

S5-3: What news sources or research do you use, and how do you utilize news items in your own trading?

Minervini: I try to keep outside influences to a bare minimum and have my trading environment as "vacuum packed" as possible, meaning there are no outside opinions coming in, just factual data. Everything I need to make buy and sell decisions is generated internally. I have subscriptions to a bunch of news sources, but I rarely use much more than earnings, sales, and margin data. You can use Yahoo Finance or Briefing.com.

Ryan: *Investor's Business Daily* is my first source, because the whole paper is designed around identifying the best growth stocks in the market. I also read the editorial page because it gives you a very conservative perspective on the news that you don't get from almost all the other news outlets. The editorials are so conservative, they make the *Wall Street Journal* look almost socialistic!

I also read the *Wall Street Journal* and the *Los Angeles Times*. Another source I scan is Briefing.com, which is an online continuous news stream. I use the news to give me additional information to size my positions or to eliminate them entirely. Scanning the news can also give me additional ideas for investments.

Zanger: I use Dow Jones, Yahoo Finance, or sometimes Ameritrade on my smartphone for news. I'm looking for upgrades, downgrades, and news du jour and most importantly checking to see how my stocks are reacting to the news. If good news is out and the stock doesn't move, maybe it's time to reduce.

Ritchie II: I generally use a combination of web-based market news including but not limited to marketwatch.com, Yahoo Finance, zacks.com, and cnbc.com. I do not have financial television on in the office, and that is a rule. I usually use the news services for stock-specific information such as earnings release dates or results, other headlines, etc. On occasion I tend to get a feel from some of the media for general sentiment.

S5-4: How many stocks do you research or review each day on average?

Minervini: I look at hundreds of charts every day, but as far as deep research into company-specific fundamentals and news, maybe a few per day. I usually know many of the names I'm following, so by the time they set up a proper buy point, I already have a beat on the story. Of course, sometimes a new stock will just come out of the blue, and we have to scurry very quickly to get up to speed.

Ryan: It depends on the market. If there are a lot of new names starting to set up, I could be very busy. I usually try to get to at least one a day.

Zanger: Each market day I review the charts of about 300 to 400 stocks, and if it's earnings season, I like to review as many earnings as I can on leading stocks. This typically requires 14 hours a day during the week and 5 to 7 hours on weekends.

Ritchie II: I probably review 300 to 500 stock charts, and I probably look at a handful (5 to 10) of stocks for more information on what they do and their fundamentals.

S5-5: Do you believe the same fundamental forces move stocks as they did many years ago?

Minervini: Absolutely! It's not a belief; it's a fact. Coca-Cola (KO) in the 1930s looked very similar to, say, Monster Beverage (MNST) in the 2000s. Coke was a small high-growth company at the time with huge earnings and a great chart pattern; few people had heard of the Coca-Cola Company back then. In the 1980s, Wal-Mart (WMT) was a small company that traded less than 50,000 shares per day. The founder

Sam Walton used to stand on a soapbox in front of the stores greeting people. Now the stock trades 7 million shares per day, and the company generates revenue in excess of $100 billion per quarter. Earnings that are driven by sales drive large stock moves. Always has been, always will be.

Ryan: Yes, and it is all about earnings growth or the expectation of earnings growth. That will never change because everyone wants to own part of a company that's becoming more valuable, and that is achieved with increased earnings.

Zanger: Earnings still drive stocks, as do interest rates and Fed liquidity. It will always be the same.

Ritchie II: This is hard for me to answer because I wasn't trading many years ago, but I will say that I don't believe stocks trade on reality in the short term. However, in the long term if a stock is going to have a big move to the upside, I think fundamentals will ultimately be driving it. A stock will not be able to sustain a large advance without continued earnings and sales expansion.

S5-6: What fundamental criteria do you look for when shorting a stock?

Minervini: Earnings deceleration could tip you off that a stock may be topping. If a stock gets hit really hard on an earnings report, I will sometimes short a subsequent dead cat bounce, if the technicals show the stock is in a stage 3 topping phase, or better yet, in a stage 4 decline.

Ryan: When I short, I put a much greater weight on the technical aspects of a stock. Many of the best shorts show technical characteristics of a top long before the fundamentals actually change. I have seen a 50% decline in a stock's price before the next earnings were even reported. If a stock forms a top that lasts longer than three months, then you should see a slowdown in the sales and earnings.

Zanger: I don't short that much, though decelerating earnings is the key to shorting stocks. I have had some major winners shorting, with one very massive short play in 2004 when I was short 160,000 shares of eBay (EBAY). In January, at presplit pricing of $105, it missed earnings and guided lower. The stock gapped down $20 in the blink of an eye on weaker-than-expected earnings and cascaded lower during the next few weeks.

Earnings were already decelerating before that point, and the stock had recently broken down from a high-level channel at the $120 area on considerable volume. Then it hit the 100-day moving average line around the $105 area and tried to bounce on heavy capitulation volume. After a brief bounce, it started fading down hard again over the next few days before earnings. I can't recall the last time a stock was breaking down so fast on such massive volume into earnings before then or since. This was my biggest short gain ever and my biggest one-day gain on a single stock ever.

I should note that there have only been a few times I've held stocks through an earnings release, and I was short in each of those few times—and got very lucky. It's been more than 10 years since I've held any stock long or short through earnings.

Ritchie II: I don't look at much fundamental data for shorting as much as technical. Either way, I rarely short, although a stock that has had explosive earnings, but whose earnings and sales are beginning to flatline or stall, is a good place to start looking. However, I would never short on those criteria alone. The technical picture would have to support the short position.

S5-7: How do you measure earnings momentum?

Minervini: There are several things I look for with regard to earnings. I look for year-over-year quarterly earnings that are accelerating sequentially during the most recent one to four quarters. Also, if a company's earnings suddenly break out of a range that is has been in for several years, that's another positive sign. If earnings start to accelerate above the growth rate, that would also get my attention.

Ryan: I look at the quarterly earnings and not only against the same quarter a year before, but I also look to see if there is any acceleration in those earnings (year-over-year) from the last two to three quarters just reported. I want to see that the earnings are really increasing dramatically. A great example of that currently is Ambarella, Inc. (AMBA). Its last four quarters of earnings show an acceleration going from 19% to 42% to 84% to a 162% increase in its most recent quarter. Its sales were also accelerating at the same time. That is the type of momentum I like to see.

Zanger: Percentage change from the same quarter same time last year is how I do it, and most momentum traders do it as well. Each quarterly earnings percentage change should be greater than each prior quarter and larger than the same quarter a year ago. Of course, gains of 30–40% or more are what many momentum traders are looking for. The larger the gains, the more likely you have a big fish on the line.

Ritchie II: I don't measure it in a mechanical sense, but I like to see explosive growth, because that tells you that something is really happening with the company that could sustain a big stock move.

S5-8: Do you require strong or accelerating sales growth?

Minervini: It would be great to have both accelerating earnings and sales. But as I said before, life isn't perfect, so you don't always get that combination. However, I would warn that if a stock is showing decent earnings growth but negative sales, it will have a limited life span. To keep earnings going strong, you will at some point need sales to kick in. A term you may have heard called "productivity enhancements" can only help a company's earnings for so long. Eventually you need top-line growth.

Ryan: In almost all cases, the sales and earnings are accelerating at the same time. A company can't keep up earnings growth for too long if its revenue isn't also growing. To Mark's point, a company can only cut costs and raise productivity for so long.

Zanger: Earnings growth is far easier for me to understand compared with sales growth. But a combination of strong earnings and sales growth is a proven formula for higher stock prices. It's hard to fully compute the valuation of stocks that have growing revenues only, like Amazon.com (AMZN) or Salesforce.com (CRM). I usually leave those stocks for others. Also, I have never forgotten that most stocks that ran hard during the Internet bubble had good strong revenue growth but little to no earnings, and price-to-earnings (P/E) multiples back then were north of 1,000. Of course, we know in hindsight that most of those companies failed and are no longer in business.

Ritchie II: I don't require it, but I certainly would like to see it.

S5-9: Do you utilize profit margins or return on equity (ROE) in your analysis?

Minervini: Yes. I like to see expanding profit margins. This can sometimes be the catalyst behind a company showing improving earnings but with negative sales. But like I said, you can only improve earnings for so long without sales. Return on equity is something that you should use to compare your stock with other stocks in the same industry group. Generally speaking, the better stocks will have a ROE of 15–17% or higher.

Ryan: They are both important figures to look at and something I make note of as I study further the profitability of a company.

Zanger: Sometimes I look at margins, but never return on equity. I pay little attention to either, as the market knows what it likes, and it's the behavior of each stock that guides me into winners.

Ritchie II: I don't look at return on equity at all. I do look at margins and like to see them increasing, but this is a bit of a secondary indicator. It's nice to see, but at some point you are going to have to sell more of whatever it is you're producing to really move the earnings and the stock price.

S5-10: Momentum stocks tend to be high-growth and high-P/E names. Do you ever find low-P/E momentum stocks?

Minervini: I rarely concern myself with the P/E ratio. As a matter of fact, I would rather invest in a name with a relatively high P/E than an ultralow P/E. At least with a high P/E, you know there's something going on and there's some demand. When a stock trades at an excessively low P/E, it could be an indication that something is really wrong. Of course, with a very high P/E, there's little room for error, so it's important to move out of the name if things start to turn sour.

Ryan: Not often do you find a momentum stock with a low P/E. These stocks tend to be slower-growing companies that all of a sudden show some tremendous earnings acceleration, and the market is just starting to recognize it.

Zanger: Not really, though there have been a few stocks over my 25-year trading career that have done well, such as Apple Inc. (AAPL), that have moved up 400 points or so while their P/E never got over 20. There have been times when the stocks in a sector, such as the semiconductor stocks back in the early 1990s, were trading at low P/Es as a group, and then they started to move up from P/Es of 10–20 to P/Es of 40–60 and with some moving even higher. As we got closer to the Internet rage (late 1990s), they went even higher as demand for computers to get connected to the Internet turned into a full tsunami. This lifted all boats in that industry to historic valuations with P/Es exceeding 100 and much higher for some of those semiconductor stocks. But as a general rule, low P/E stocks (8–20) usually stay low and move slowly.

Ritchie II: I never look at P/E—so I really can't answer that with any certainty.

S5-11: What's more important, current quarterly earnings growth or the long-term growth rate? Or do you require both, or neither, to enter a trade?

Minervini: The only time I concern myself with the long-term growth rate is when I compare current earnings to get an idea if growth is accelerating versus the historical numbers. With regard to future growth, no one knows what the long-term growth of a company will be—not even the CEO—and past growth is simply looking in the rearview mirror. Focus on current quarterly growth. Most of the better stocks will show current growth rates accelerating faster than previous growth.

Ryan: The best situation is if you have both current quarterly earnings growth and a strong long-term growth rate. I would put the greater emphasis on the quarterly earnings acceleration though, because that would include stocks that might be in a turnaround situation.

Zanger: Most all of my big winners had very large earnings growth in the current quarter and in the past three to four quarters.

Ritchie II: I don't require either, but I look at the most recent three to four quarters as well as where the trend is on a yearly basis. So if the stock has a good few recent quarters and is on pace to make more for the year than, say, the last four to five years, I take that as a very good sign.

SECTION SIX

General Market

S6-1: Can you apply your trading method to indexes or just stocks?

Minervini: I trade stocks because this gives me leverage on the indexes. If the Nasdaq moves up 10%, leading stocks could move up 5 to 10 times that amount during the same time frame.

Ryan: You can apply these methods to indexes and exchange-traded funds (ETFs), but I mainly focus on individual stocks.

Zanger: Trading chart patterns with volume apply to everything and anything that trades, from stocks to commodities to indexes to currencies.

Ritchie II: You can certainly apply some of the same principles; however, the indexes themselves are far more efficiently priced and noisy than individual stocks, so they are much more prone to whipsaw action and aberrant volatility that can jerk you around. I have at times, when I'm very bullish and feel underinvested, taken a decent position in the index—although I only do this if I feel we're at a very low-risk point where I can do so with a really tight stop. However, I usually like to trade stocks, because if the market is really good, then even being in one really good name will be far better than trading the index.

S6-2: Do you try to time the overall market as a guide to your trading? Do you have some market gauge or indicator that you track?

Minervini: Not really. I have a general market risk model that does a pretty good job of getting me in and out near market turning points, but my main focus is on the individual stocks. If there are no stocks to trade, it doesn't really matter what some indicator or model says.

Ryan: I use a few different indicators to time the market, but you have to be careful not to let the general market get you too bearish or bullish as to influence what is happening with your individual stocks. You could get a sell signal from market indicators, but if your stocks are holding up well, you shouldn't sell them. You probably heard that saying, "Don't throw the baby out with the bathwater." You want to watch the general market but not to the point that you sell all your stocks when your indicators flash a downtrend.

Zanger: There's no magic indicator out there other than the charts and the leading stocks, along with how they are behaving. Chart patterns and price behavior are everything to me.

Ritchie II: There are some general market indicators I watch, like the overall advance-decline line, new highs and lows, overall volume on the general market, sentiment, etc. However, I don't use any of them as a timing mechanism but more as secondary indicators. I usually never buy the general market on the long side; at times I will short it but not because of any one indicator. Together my trading and the universe of stocks I'm watching create the primary indicator I look at. Sometimes that indicator is highly correlated to how the general market is moving, and sometimes it's quite different.

S6-3: How do you select which stocks to sell when you have a new market sell signal?

Minervini: I just let the stocks signpost which ones I should sell. This happens either if I get stopped out or if I have a decent gain in a name; in which case I'll choke off the trade so I get stopped at a point that I lock in a majority of the profit when a pullback occurs. After I initiate a trade, I wait for one or the other to take place.

Stock trading is about anticipating coming movements and then waiting to be proved right or wrong. Even if I turn bearish on the market while I'm holding longs, I will usually let the stocks stop me out. I don't usually sell everything on my "opinion" of the market. I simply tighten my stops and let the price action take me out of the positions one by one. Very often a handful of my stocks will hold their stops, and I'll even get through a market pullback still holding names I had before the correction began.

Ryan: The stocks that I have a loss on are the first to go. If they haven't performed well since I bought them, they are probably not going to act well in a poor market environment. If the whole market is starting to roll over, I will work up the order from weakest to strongest, selling them off or reducing positions. I want to hold on to my best stocks as long as possible because they might resist most of the market decline and then continue higher when the next uptrend begins.

Zanger: When I have a new market sell signal, I sell everything at once, even the kitchen sink if I can pry it loose from the wall. Why wait for a stock to move lower to sell it? Sell it now before it plunges with the market.

Ritchie II: I don't trade on market buy or sell signals; if a stock hits my stop level, then I sell it.

S6-4: When the market turns sour, are you inclined to take profits on marginal winners, set breakeven stops, or wait and let your original stop loss get hit?

Minervini: If I feel the market is in real trouble, I usually start moving stops to breakeven levels on marginal winners, and I choke off big winners with backstops. I try to allow my stocks to go through the first "natural reaction" (pullback). I may just sell the stocks that get into trouble or those that have gotten well ahead of themselves. With all that said, it's still a judgment call and a balancing act, and that's why trading is an art.

Ryan: If I feel the market has entered a downtrend, I will take profits on my marginal winners to cut my invested position. The first stocks to go in my portfolio as the market turns down are the ones with losses, then the ones with marginal gains, and lastly the best and strongest stocks in my portfolio.

Zanger: When the market turns a bit sour versus taking a hard break, I'm more inclined to reduce 60–80% and then see what the market wants to do. If it regains its footing, I will add back strong stocks at very selective areas.

Ritchie II: This is really different depending upon where I think the overall market is and how my trading has been going. If I'm coming on the heels of a difficult period, I'm more apt to just tighten everything up or cut and run altogether.

S6-5: If an uptrending chart looks great but we're in a downtrending market, do you buy the stock or remain on the sidelines?

Minervini: If I have evidence that we are in a correction or, worse, in a bear market, I will generally stay on the sidelines or, at the very least, trade lighter than normal. If I see signs of accumulation in the major averages and stocks are setting up constructively according to my criteria, I will take some small "pilot buys." However, I don't usually step up my trading much until I see a second wave of stocks set up subsequent to the first wave—and provided that the my pilot buys show some progress and the second wave starts to emerge. In most cases, I want to see additional follow-through in the averages around the same time. Most importantly, I want to gain some traction and see progress with my initial commitments. Once I see that things are working, I step on the gas and ramp up my exposure pretty quickly.

Ryan: If the stock has all the characteristics that I look for even in a downtrending market, I will go ahead and buy the stock. There are times even in the worst of bear markets where a company is in a strong growth phase and its stock can buck the trend in a down market. But there are very few stocks that can do that, so you have to be very selective.

U.S. Surgical is one example that continued to make new highs when the market rolled over in July 1990 and dropped over 20% into October 1990 during the Iraqi invasion of Kuwait. U.S. Surgical made a series of higher bases and moved from $24 to $34 during that same time period. The stock then exploded to the upside when the weight of the market came off, and the stock moved from the mid-$30s to over $130.

Zanger: The overall market trend is the compass showing me true north, so I avoid stocks 90% of the time when the market is in a downtrend. However, if it's just a market swoon of 2–3%, then I would step into a leading stock that is breaking out while the market is in this modest dip down.

There are rare circumstances when you can go against the overall trend; this is the case with gold, which often moves up when the market is trending down, or with a bear ETF stock that is moving up when the market is trending down. Growth and momentum stocks are usually moving with the overall market.

Ritchie II: A declining market is not reason enough by itself for me to not take a trade. In general though, if there is only one stock that is holding up during a decline, I'm usually not inclined to buy it; I want to see a variety of stocks that look attractive potentially bucking the general market trend in order for me to be really interested.

S6-6: How do you determine if the market is under distribution or accumulation, and how do you use this with respect to your trading?

Minervini: If the market is selling off and volume is expanding, that would indicate distribution and the opposite for accumulation. I look to see if my stocks are confirming this action.

Ryan: I watch the relationship between the price and volume action in the major indexes. That influences the percentage that I should be invested. If the market is starting to have some big down days on increased volume, that might cause me to cut back on the size and number of the positions I might have in the portfolio.

Zanger: I use an audio program that I wrote for myself back in 2000, and it gives me a "sound picture" of how the trades are clustering and their frequency. The program is called IQXP. com, and this sound system is just a small portion in this program that I had written and installed by the owner of IQXP.

I put in about 12 stocks and then listen to the market all day. If the bids are being hit, then it makes a coconut sound; or if the ask is being hit, it makes a hammer sound. If I hear a preponderance of coconuts going off for a few days or weeks, then I know distribution is taking place; and if there are hammers going for days on end, then I know buyers are all around.

Ritchie II: I just look at the NYSE and Nasdaq Composite indexes and see if their most recent advances or declines have been on higher-than-average volume. The most important factor for me is to not see heavy selling if I'm starting to go long, because it potentially means the wind is not at my back.

S6-7: What overall market analysis gets you to invest more aggressively in the market? How do you know when to step on the gas?

Minervini: My stock purchases show gains. That's really my main gauge. If stocks set up, I take some positions. If things are working, I get more aggressive. When my stock trades are not working well, I cut back my exposure and the number of commitments. This is a very simple method but very effective. If you scale up when trades are working and scale back when things are not working well, you ensure that you will be trading your largest when trading your best and trading your smallest when trading your worst. This is how you make big money and avoid big losses.

Ryan: If I see a number of stocks breaking into new high ground and new leadership, then that will probably lead me to see this as a whole new up leg in the market. That would give me the confidence to invest more.

Zanger: Recognizing very positive chart patterns is the key to getting more aggressive, as is analyzing earnings and what the Fed is doing. When you have this complete package of skills, then you will know when it's time to step on the gas. Stocks are usually strongest in the first few years of Fed easing and when earnings growth starts to appear after a recession.

Ritchie II: The only thing that gets me to really step up my exposure is my actual trading. It doesn't matter how many indicators or even how many stocks look good; if I'm not making money, I'm not going to get more aggressive without some traction first.

S6-8: If you see a leading stock break out from a sound chart pattern before the market experiences an IBD follow-through day (FTD), do you buy it? If yes, do you buy a full position before a follow-through day happens, or are you more conservative?

Minervini: The time when a follow-through day is essential is after a bear market or a good-size correction. This is when you want to see big volume come in as the market comes off the bottom and starts a new up leg. However, I rely more on the individual stocks than any index, indicator, or news item. Even if the major indexes bottom, that doesn't mean individual stocks are ready to move up in earnest. And then there are times when leading stocks start to move well in advance of the final market low. So, yes, I will buy stocks even before an FTD occurs.

I look at it this way: if the market looks great, but there are no stocks setting up that meet my criteria, I'm not buying anything anyway. So the stocks have the final word. I think most traders would do much better if they completely ignored the "market" or the major indexes and just focused on the stocks themselves. I have always been pretty good at calling market turns, even though, ironically, I don't try to call market turns. You would be amazed at how great your market calls can be when you tune out the "market" and tune into the stocks.

Ryan: I might start with a 5% position instead of a 10% position if the market isn't in an uptrend. I would quickly add to the position if it continues to follow through. You have to realize that the leading stocks in many cases break out sometimes months before the market starts into an uptrend.

Zanger: Buying before a follow-through day would depend on the stock's prior strength and other factors, such as when earnings come out, what the earnings are, how liquid the stock happens to be, and how other stocks in the market are behaving. I would say yes, I would buy a leader well before an FTD, provided it has high volume and amazing earnings.

However, I most likely would not buy a full position and might get 50% long and then wait for more conviction in other leading stocks or a follow-through day before loading up. Let's not forget that many follow-through days fail, so it's not the cure-all it's cracked up to be.

Ritchie II: If I am coming out of cash or a very defensive position, I always employ a "toe-in-the-water" mentality first. I will buy before a general market confirmation, but usually with smaller-than-normal exposure; but as soon as a position or two begins to work, I look to step up my exposure and risk tolerance rather quickly.

SECTION SEVEN

Entry Criteria

S7-1: What aspects of a stock would really grab your attention as a potential buy?

Minervini: From a fundamental standpoint, earnings breaking out of a range and accelerating. I look for quarterly acceleration and a "breakout year." I also want to see sales increasing. As far as the technicals are concerned, I want to own stocks that are holding up relatively well coming out of sound bases through low-risk entry points.

Ryan: I like to see that the stock has had the ability to have a strong move in the past. Many times I am not buying a stock on its first move up, but on its second or third move. I would also like to see a very tight base with a small price range and dry-up in volume. Combine that with great fundamentals and part of a strong group, and that would get my attention.

Zanger: A great-moving stock in a strong group with superior earnings and revenue growth will grab my attention every time. Show me this stock combined with a fabulous chart pattern, and I will back up the truck when it leaves the basing area.

Ritchie II: I want to see a stock that looks to be under accumulation that has good earnings and sales on the table. So technically it should be in a long-term uptrend that is supported by volume and then consolidating in an orderly manner.

S7-2: Do you buy the full position all at once, or do you buy partially and add in increments; and do you scale out when a stock moves against you, or do you just sell it all at once?

Minervini: Sometimes I will buy a tiny amount just to keep my finger on the pulse of the market with real money at risk and then scale in from there if things progress. But once my trades start working, I go right in with full-size positions. When my trading is working well, I like to run racks like a pool player on a roll. But most of the time, I'm moving in incrementally and feeling things out. If I'm going to scale in, I sometimes will wait until near the end of the day to see if the stock is going to close strong before adding.

Ryan: I always scale in and out of a position. On the day I buy a stock, I might first buy a 5% position, and as we get into the last hour of trading, I increase it to 10%. If it doesn't have a strong close, I would wait for the next day to see if there is any follow-through. If there is, I will quickly move it to 10%. When I sell, I usually scale out of a position unless it is breaking all sorts of support; then I sell it all at once.

Zanger: If the stock has had super earnings and is gapping up quickly after hours, I might try to buy shares if I can get within 5% of the base. The next day and after the earnings conference call, I might add and double the shares and see how the stock is holding up. The hope is that the stock can sit for a week or so and create a bull flag or channel, and then I might add.

Scaling in is typical for people trading size, because it's all about liquidity. When a stock is breaking out and volume is heavy, I buy maybe 40% of what I would like to have. Should volume and price behavior continue to be favorable, I might add another 20% or so later in the day. I usually wait until the next day or two before adding the balance, but if the stock rests the day after I bought it, I might hold off on adding the balance until the stock can reaccelerate from a small base and confirm with new highs.

Should the stock stall out instead, I will reduce in reverse manner of what I noted above. In some instances I will dump everything rather than scale out, if, for example, the stock is cracking down hard or becoming sloppy.

Ritchie II: I usually try and scale in, but much of this depends upon how my trading has been going as well as the technical setup. If I feel I may be buying a name early, then I will always buy a smaller line and look to add. I will only buy a "full" position right away if trading is going well and I particularly like the situation. For selling, I will generally scale down if it's a larger position, but if the stop is tight and I know I want out, I have no problem cutting it all at once.

S7-3: Are you buying the breakout a certain amount above the breakout price intraday, or do you wait for the closing daily price?

Minervini: I buy intraday. Once the pivot point is breached, I'm in—usually a few pennies to as much as 20–30 cents above my buy point.

Ryan: When I set a spot where the stock is breaking out, I buy 1 cent above that price. I might start with a small position as it is breaking out intraday, wait for a close in the upper half of that day's trading range, and then buy the rest of the position. If it is a perfect base and the volume is strong, then I will buy it intraday. If it looks like it will close near its high on a big pickup in volume, I will add to get a 5–10% position the first day.

Zanger: The stock could be long gone if I wait for a closing price. I use the first 10–20 cents above the breakout or pivot area to start my buying and see how the stock reacts and then add relentlessly if the stock has volume and the overall market is just starting to move.

Let's not forget that stocks on late-stage bases near the end of a market move fail far too often to trade large size, so if you have to buy one of these late-stage bases, buy small positions so as not to get pummeled if they fail. Putting together a package of market stages and stock stages works best. Sometimes I have to sit out the market for two to six months with no trades, waiting for the big trade opportunities to come along.

The biggest mistake traders make is thinking they have to make a few trades every day. While this might work for a few skilled traders with a few thousand shares here and there, it's not where the big money is made, at least not for me. To trade large sizes you need a stock that has built a super base and then explodes on millions of shares traded per day. It should continue to trade with the same level of impressive volume day in and day out for a month to three months.

Ritchie II: I almost never wait for a close to buy, although I generally like to see the stock close above the breakout level if there is a clear technical price point. I will often set an alarm at a level that I think is important and then see how the stock acts before I put on a position. If I'm buying, I don't generally want to see a ton of shares for sale, because if there's lots of stock for sale, the trade probably isn't ready to move with any real conviction.

S7-4: How do you go from cash to fully invested?

Minervini: I let the stocks guide me. If stocks are setting up and moving through buy points, I buy them one by one until I'm fully invested. I try not to wait for my "favorites." Often while you wait for a particular stock to emerge, you miss the boat on real market leaders that are blasting off. You want to be neutral and agnostic. Trust the charts and your research, and buy the stocks that meet your criteria. Your opinion will always cost you money in the long run.

Ryan: It all depends on how many stocks I can find to buy and the market itself. If I feel the market has turned, but I can't find 10 stocks to buy, I might get exposure by buying a position in the SPYs or QQQs. Then I'll peel those ETFs off as I find stocks that are breaking out.

Zanger: Following the most liquid high-beta stocks makes it easy to get fully invested quickly. If the market is coming out of a correction, you have plenty of time to scale in. If I get 80% invested in two or three days, that is a serious move for me. I would only consider going all in on margin these days on extremely powerful market moves, which happen rarely.

Ritchie II: This to me is where the skill has to be learned and honed, and it's the number one area I'm still trying to improve upon. In my experience, when you are coming out of a cash position, you have the most potential risk and opportunity at the same time. The only way to tell the difference is to let the market action tell you.

If I buy two names and both of them immediately start following through, then I get more aggressive and step up my size and exposure. Likewise, if the first things I buy don't follow through or even stop me out, then I'm going to do the opposite. If you let the market take your exposure up and down, you'll always do better than if you arbitrarily decide; and in my experience the more aggressive you get on the heels of initial success, the better off you'll be.

S7-5: How do you manage to trade many stocks? What if, say, 4 or 5 out of 15 you are watching break out at the same time?

Minervini: In more than 30 years of trading, I have never had five stocks break out at exactly the same time. Sometimes a few will break out very close to each other. Of course, you can always use limit buy-stop orders preset at breakout levels.

Ryan: I have alerts set on all the stocks that I am interested in buying or adding to. If they all break out at the same time,

I buy them in order of strongest potential based on earnings and past price performance.

Zanger: I trade everything with verbal market orders to my broker these days, and I don't use limit orders. I've used multiple brokers and multiple platforms in the past to move quickly when needed. We have used algorithms (algos) like Sonar through the GS platform and RediPlus and Baytrade's platform with the BTIG brokerage. In the end, I prefer to trade manually because it helps me get a better feel for the stocks' price behavior. My broker and I have our system down, and we can move fast enough to get me to where I need to be most of the time.

Ritchie II: I set an alarm to alert me to anything that I think looks buyable, because I want to see how many stocks in my universe are acting well as they hit what I think are important price points. In addition, there are names that I often go into the day knowing I want to buy and others that I may buy depending upon what my overall exposure is and how my trading is going.

If it's a name that I have decided is a must-buy, then I buy it regardless; and if more names are breaking out than I can afford to buy based upon my risk tolerance or cash available, then I generally buy those that are ranked highest based on my criteria.

Finally, I will sometimes consider jockeying for position by selling part or all of a name that isn't working in favor of one that I like more that is breaking out. However, I try and let the stocks determine what to buy. In my experience, if I just buy what's working, I usually don't wind up too far off.

S7-6: How do you define your entry point?

Minervini: I'm looking for what Livermore referred to as the line of least resistance to develop; that's a trading range that matures to a point when supply stops coming to market. When you have a limited amount of supply and big demand for the shares, you get explosive price action.

Ryan: I have a couple of entry points. One is when the stock is near its highs, and another is when the stock has pulled back. When a stock is breaking out, I buy it when it is breaking above most of its recent trading range. It doesn't necessarily have to be the exact new high, but it needs to be above 90–95% of the trading range formed near the new high. The other buy point is when a stock has pulled back and is turning up but is no more than about 15% off its high. At that buy spot, I use a few more technical indicators such as moving averages, trendlines, and momentum readings.

Zanger: An all-time new high is usually my best entry area on a massive surge in volume. If the market happens to be coming off oversold areas or a market correction, you have to target key reversal bars or descending channels or wedges for those entries.

Ritchie II: If you were to examine most of my trades, you would see a majority of them being executed in the direction of the trend, within 5% of new 52-week highs, and at times where the stock has been correcting in a shorter-term time frame.

S7-7: Do you ever trade a stock that you took a recent loss on? What is your reentry plan?

Minervini: Yes, I often reenter a stock that previously stopped me out, but only if the stock sets up another low-risk entry point. I don't just take a stock off my list because it stops me out. This is why you should have various setups and techniques for entry. It's like having a toolbox: you don't build a house with just a hammer; you have all sorts of tools to get the job done. I break down reset patterns into two groups: (1) pivot-failure resets and (2) base-failure resets. Pivot failures can recover very quickly, sometimes in just a few days. Base failures take longer, usually weeks to months depending on how severe the break is.

Ryan: I have been stopped out a couple of times in a name only to come back the third time and have a huge winner. My reentry is when the stock again sets up technically. I might have bought the stock as it was first breaking out, but it failed and came back into the base. If the stock then spends more time rebuilding and cleaning up the base, I will try it again as it goes to highs for the second or third attempt out of the base.

Zanger: I do and have many times. Generally I like to see the stock reset its base, which could be a few weeks to a month or more. I would not, for example, reenter the stock within a few days of exiting, as it's clearly having trouble at the breakout area at that time.

Ritchie II: Absolutely. In general, I think a major difference between pros and novice traders is the way they think about a particular market that hasn't treated them well. For example, pros have no problem stepping into a stock or market that they've lost on a few times in a row, whereas novices try once, and if they aren't successful, they give up. They may think that a particular market or stock has it "in" for them. In my style, I can sometimes be right but be too early or too tight on my stop, and so as long as the name doesn't break down hard, I will keep it on the radar for reentry.

S7-8: How do you deal with being shaken out of a trade only to see it go on to hit your original entry price again later in the day?

Minervini: I will sometimes go back into a name that stops me out intraday. It really depends on how it's trading. This is based on intraday action, so it's more on a feel for the "tape."

Ryan: I would look to see if I had placed my stop too close to my entry. If it happens in one day, then the stock may be very volatile and not a stock I can stomach. Sometimes volatile stocks require too much "eyeball time" and are best left to other investors. If the stock sets up again, I can always buy it back.

Zanger: That doesn't happen often these days, though there have been a few cases over the years. Most of those cases were back in the Internet bubble days when I traded a fewer number of shares and I would sell out with a very tight stop and reenter when the stock made a new daily high.

Of course, you have to watch these sorts of trades very closely, or they can eat you up. In those days, if you were right, the stock might soar $12–$25 on a gap up the next day and then subsequently add $50 or more the following few days.

Ritchie II: I rarely ever reenter a trade I have gotten knocked out of the same day; usually I reassess and wait a day or two. Sometimes I will reduce and add back a piece of a name, but if I've completely liquidated something, I will almost always wait until the next day.

S7-9: Do you think a trader should enter momentum stocks using pullbacks to moving averages (MA)?

Minervini: I will sometimes buy on a pullback to a moving average such as the 20-day or the 50-day. I generally will only buy on pullbacks to moving averages the first or second time after a breakout from a sound consolidation period. However, even if I do buy on a pullback, I only buy as the stock turns up and never as the stock is falling. I want to see the stock moving in the direction of my trade. Keep in mind, if trading were as easy as just buying a pullback to a moving average, everyone would be rich stock traders. It's a very obvious and basic way to trade, and at times it can be profitable, especially in leading stocks at the beginning of a bull move.

Ryan: Yes, you can buy pullbacks, but it doesn't necessarily have to be to a moving average. I have found some indicators such as MACD and stochastics to tell me when a stock is ready to turn up from a pullback. I watch the price and volume characteristics as the stock pulls back to give me another indication the pullback is over. Buying pullbacks is a bit more complicated than buying breakouts.

Zanger: It would be an ideal situation to get a strong stock to pull back to the 10-day or 21-day simple moving average line. I find the stocks with the best momentum find support at these moving average lines and bounce from there. The 50-day and 150-day MA can be good too, but for me the 10-day and 21-day MA lines are best when considering a stock on a pullback.

Ritchie II: Sure, as long as they have a plan or idea for what they expect the stock to do at the average. For example, I won't blindly put in a limit bid for a stock at or near its moving average, but I may look to see how it acts in reference to an average and then buy it after it has bounced off it.

If you blindly buy, you are guaranteed to be in every losing situation where the average is not supportive. If you wait for a bounce, you avoid the "falling-knife" situations; you may have to pay up a bit, but that price is often more favorable in terms of probability of trade success than the lower price.

S7-10: Could you give advice on adding to your winners?

Minervini: I'm not as big on adding to your winners as much as I am on timing the purchase just right with an optimal position size in the first place. I will add if I started with a smaller-than-normal position and then a new low-risk entry presents itself subsequent to my initial entry. I will often start my position early in the day and then ramp up my exposure to a full-size position if the stock closes strong during the last 15 to 30 minutes of the day.

Ryan: It is all determined by the price action after my initial purchase. If it follows through on good volume, I will probably be adding to my position. If it stalls and has poor closes on weak volume, then there is no reason to increase the position. I only add to stocks on which I already have a profit.

In a year, you really only need one or two really good stocks to have great performance, but you must handle them right. You must add to a stock after it has built a new base following its first move up. You can add to it again on subsequent bases. On a longer move, you can build the size of the position into 20–25% of your portfolio. A position of that size should only be achieved through price appreciation and by adding more on subsequent bases.

Zanger: Adding to a winner is basically averaging up. If the stock takes a quick break on a downgrade or a secondary stock offering, I could be underwater in a flash. Just buy right at the pivot point or a hair above it if volume and the market are good, and hang on for the ride. Sell on the way up into strength and volume. The Street must be very hungry for the stock and pushing the stock price up rapidly with massive volume. This would be a stock I would be buying heavily on the breakout and then adding more after a few days of rest.

Ritchie II: I think until you've done it successfully a number of times, you don't really see its importance. Most people tend to be backward looking by nature in terms of almost all experiences. So when you own something at a lower price, the idea of buying more at a higher price feels wrong, because you think "I should have just bought more at the lower price when I had the chance."

In terms of my own trade, if I only added when prices were back to even or below my entries, I would have eliminated almost all my best trades—and added to many of my worst. You have to really wrap your mind around this idea and then see it in action a number of times before it really starts to sink in; the idea is to pyramid in such a way where you don't add much more risk but use your gains to finance buying more and really torque your overall risk-reward to the upside.

S7-11: Do you buy gaps? If yes, what if the gap opens past your buy point?

Minervini: As a general rule, I don't chase gaps. If a stock gaps up more than a few percentage points past my buy point, I won't touch it. The type of gap trade I do like is when a stock gaps out of a large base on an earnings report and I get in not too far above the pivot point. If the earnings are really good, the stock should move even higher and put me at a profit right away. This occurred on July 26, 2012, and also on February 16, 2012, when Cabela's (CAB) reported earnings (see Chart 7.1).

On the other hand, if the stock gaps under the prior day's low, that's going in the wrong direction and would then

Chart 7.1   Cabela's (CAB), 2012

have to put in an "outside day" or what is called a "bullish engulfing pattern" to break out on the same day. If a stock gaps unexpectedly, I'm careful not to jump in with a knee-jerk reaction. I come in with a plan, and I want to see things happen as I envision. I don't like surprises, and I rarely react to them.

Ryan: I rarely buy gaps past my buy point, and only if the stock has spectacular fundamental characteristics. I some-times wait toward the end of the day to see where in the day's range the stock closed. If it had a strong close, I might buy it and set a stop at the low of the day. If it doesn't, I might wait to see if it can go through the high of the gap day. It usually will move through the gap day high in the next few days; if not, I keep watching it and wait for it to set up a proper base.

Zanger: Yes, I do buy gaps unless the gap is too far past my buy point. Usually I would not buy the stock if it's up more than 5% above my buy point. In these high-gap situations, I will wait until a small minibase sets up and then buy as it moves above that pivot area on volume.

I should add, there have been a few stocks, a very few stocks, where I have broken my own rules—for example, during a massive beat of earnings for a large global-scale company such as a Facebook (FB) or a Google Inc. (GOOG) shortly after going public. I would not "back up the truck" on the initial gap up but instead buy about 20% of what I normally would and see what kind of action we get the next day. If things look solid, I will pick up most of my shares on the second, third, or even fourth day, should the stock hold its gap well.

On April 22, 2014, I bought Netflix right after earnings were reported when the stock gapped up on the open. That day the stock closed at the midpoint of its daily range. The very next day the price reversed and closed right on the low; I sold some that day. When the stock continued lower the next day, I closed out the position and took about a 6% loss on the trade. Looking back, it was a poor setup that I forced too early.

Ritchie II: I rarely buy gaps, although there are two scenarios when I will buy a gap. The first is when the price gaps past my intended breakout area but not too far that would make my stop too wide, so usually only a few percentage points. The other scenario is where I will buy a gap with a very tight stop on an earnings announcement that I believe is absolutely phenomenal and where I believe there is a chance for a very rapid price appreciation.

SECTION EIGHT

Risk Management

S8-1: How do you determine the placement of stops on your trades?

Minervini: If a technical level coincides with acceptable risk, then I try to hold the stock until the chart sours. But in volatile names where there's too much risk, I simply use a percentage stop. I sometimes just back into a fixed dollar amount of risk and position size accordingly.

Ryan: It is usually a percentage loss or just below an area where the stock had recently had support. It's best when there's a nice base just below my buy spot because that provides me a very definite price to get out.

Zanger: On my charts I extend rising trendlines along the bottoms of the daily bars as a first step for determining reasonable stops. Then I look for relatively fast-moving averages like the 10-day or 21-day. When one of these areas is broken, I usually sell out or reduce.

Ritchie II: I start from my trading metrics, specifically in regard to my win-loss relationship. So on a percentage basis, I calculate what will help me maintain a good weighted-average win-loss relationship on my trades, which usually dictates that I need to average in the mid-single digits in terms of a percentage stop. In addition, if I'm buying correctly and the market is acting well, the charts usually start to break down somewhere between 3% and 10% below my buy points.

S8-2: Is there a maximum percentage of total equity you would cap your risk at?

Minervini: Yes, I don't want to risk more than 2.5% of my equity. But on average, I risk 0.75–1.25% of my total equity per trade. A simple way to understand this would be if you bought a 25% position and set your stop loss at 10%, then that would be risking 2.5% of your total equity on the trade; a 5% stop would risk 1.25% of your total equity.

Ryan: It would be a maximum of 1%, which would equate to a 10% loss on a 10% position. I just never want any one position to cause a big setback to my whole portfolio.

Zanger: I would cap my total equity risk at 20% of my entire portfolio. On an individual stock, I would try to cap my risk at 1–3%.

Ritchie II: Yes, but it is determined by a number of factors. The first and most important is how my trading has been going. If I've been in a losing streak or having a tougher time, the amount is usually not more than 100 basis points (BP) across the whole portfolio; then as I get my footing, I start to bump it up, in terms of either adding more positions or adding to existing ones.

If things are working well, I generally will have 200–300 BP of risk that I'm carrying; and if I have names that I've taken profits on or I know are at better than breakeven stops, I will have upward of 500 BP of open trade risk, but again that is only on the heels of success.

I don't necessarily make as hard and fast a rule when things are working as when they're not. When things aren't working, I'm not going to take on more risk, and that is a staple in my trading regardless of the market behavior, time frame, or approach.

S8-3: Even though you may set tight stops, how do you deal with the risk of gaps and holding overnight?

Minervini: Unless you go flat every night, the risk of a gap is always present. You can't eliminate the risk, but you can mitigate it. This is where position sizing comes into play. If you are buying stocks that have previously opened on huge down gaps over the past three to six months, you could be taking a much higher amount of risk by owning—if I can borrow a phrase from David Ryan, a "serial gapper." So the quality of your buys plays a big role as well. I always tell traders to sell down to the sleeping point, or what my assistant refers to as the "pillow factor." Simply put, if you can't sleep, you're trading too large.

Ryan: Overnight news or gaps are just part of the risk you have to take when trading. If you can't sleep at night worrying about a position, then you should let someone else manage your money. If earnings are about to be reported, I might cut down my position size in the stock to reduce the risk.

Zanger: Holding overnight has never been a problem for me; some of my biggest gains have come from holding overnight and over the weekend. Large gaps down are a problem, but you can usually sense when trouble is brewing and reduce during troubled times, like just before FOMC meetings or some major news coming out. I do this frequently. Don't get me wrong; I've been tagged hard on a few monster gaps down in my trading career, but in the long run, holding overnight and over the weekend during powerful bull markets has worked in my favor by a large margin.

Ritchie II: This isn't really as big an issue as it might seem, with the exception of certain headlines, like earnings. I have noticed that gap risk is very limited if the market is healthy and your selection criteria are good. It's pretty rare that a stock under accumulation will gap hard against you in a good market; however, you see just the opposite in corrective periods with higher volatility.

I use a sort of weather analogy. I'm from Chicago, and people not from the area are always saying something like "Wow, the weather there must be horrible in the winter." And the reality is that's true, but you don't go outside in shorts and a T-shirt during a blizzard. Individual stock action is similar in that it can be largely influenced by the surrounding environment.

S8-4: On setting stops, would you rather take one 10% loss or two 5% losses, giving you more chances to get the trade right?

Minervini: I would rather take smaller losses and have more chances at getting the entry correct. A 10% loss is my "uncle" point, or maximum stop, but I rarely ever see that big a loss on a trade. Keep in mind, the tighter your stop, the more accurate your timing needs to be, but the bigger the loss, the more it works against you geometrically. I would rather work on my timing than work on digging out of a hole.

Ryan: I would probably take two 5% losses because if my timing is right, the stock shouldn't drop below my 5% stop.

Zanger: Tough question to answer, as it's "six of one, half dozen of the other." Either way you've still lost 10%. I guess I would be in the 5% camp if I had to choose one.

Ritchie II: Two 5% losses; I'll always take more shots at a smaller size.

S8-5: Can you talk about a losing trade when your analysis went wrong and why?

Minervini: I hate to buy cyclical stocks and rarely do well in them, but I bought Alcoa, Inc. (AA) in November 2014. The stock went up for a few days and then came in; I sold and took a relatively small loss. The stock is down considerably from where I sold it.

Ryan: My losing trades occur when I'm not disciplined enough to stick to my rules. The emotion comes in, and I buy a stock that is too extended or whose base is not exactly set up the right way. Buying at exactly the right spot and getting up on a stock that first day are usually winning trades.

A recent losing trade was when I bought Jack in the Box (JACK) as it was breaking out to new highs on March 24, 2015. The stock had a small base after a gap up on earnings. The stock went into new highs and immediately stalled on the first day. The very next day it dropped 3.4% on volume that was heavier than the breakout volume. The lack of follow-through and the absence of positive volume doomed the stock. I sold for a 3% loss when the stock failed to rally back quickly.

My mistake was buying a stock with a small base and not getting any volume as it moved to new highs. You want to see multiple days of increased volume and higher prices to get the stock up and moving out of its base. The four-week base was also not the best setup after the long move the stock had; longer bases usually result in bigger moves.

Zanger: Most losing trades are the result of a lack of buying interest after the stock breaks out. My analysis of the bases is pretty solid, and I can identify candidates with a very impartial eye. I position within the best setups and respond to what comes; that is all any trader can do.

An example of one of my losing trades was in the biotech sector with Medivation Inc. (MDVN). The stock was surging out of a well-formed base in February 2010, and the day after I bought the stock, the company's drug was shot down by the FDA. The stock was trading at a 75% discount at the open the next morning.

Ritchie II: I recently bought a small position in Globus Medical (GMED) on February 23, 2015, as it was breaking out a few days before its earnings. The stock had a large short interest going into earnings and was close to an all-time high, so my analysis was that it might start moving ahead of the earnings as shorts would cover, and perhaps it could move largely in my favor if the announcement was good. I held into the announcement, and the stock immediately gapped up a little but then reversed hard, and I got out.

I also bought a position in Opko Health (OPK) on March 23, 2015, and it looked great initially. However, it promptly reversed hard two days later. I knew immediately that my timing was wrong, as it wasn't acting right, and I got knocked out of the trade.

S8-6: Do you scale out when a stock moves against you and you're at a loss, or do you just sell the entire position all at once?

Minervini: If my stop is hit, I sell out my entire position immediately. I will sometimes stagger my stops and come out averaging the same percentage loss as I would at one stop price, but by staggering I can have a chance at staying in part of the trade. As a result, a loss will get stopped at successively lower levels and peeled off a little at a time, usually in thirds or halves.

Ryan: I usually sell it all at once when it breaks my stop. Your first loss is always your best loss. Protecting capital is always my first goal.

Zanger: That depends on how liquid the stock is and how many shares I've purchased. In an ideal world, I would like to sell everything at the snap of my fingers and have the position be gone with one trade, but that rarely happens. If volume has dried up and the stock is cascading down, I can sell deep-in-the-money call options (calls) first, then start to sell my stock position since my selling will inevitably force down the stock price. The calls will become cheaper as I sell the stock down, and this offsets my losses as I stage my exit. By the way, an important addendum: I'm more likely to sell calls in a stock that is less liquid and trades under 2 million to 3 million shares per day; and I'm not inclined to do so in a liquid stock that trades 7 million to 50 million shares a day, where I can just sell my shares accordingly.

Ritchie II: The larger the position, the more I'm apt to scale out. If it's a small position and it hits a predetermined stop level, I'll usually just cut the whole thing, knowing I can put the trade back on if conditions change. If it's a larger position, I will usually cut it in pieces as it moves against me.

S8-7: Do you place open stop-loss orders with your broker or use mental stops? It seems like the market makers gun for stops, especially with gap-down openings.

Minervini: I generally use mental stops. At times, they can "gun for stops" if the stop is close to the current price quote. If the stop is far away on a liquid name, you should be fine.

Ryan: I only place my stops intraday and don't like to leave them in overnight. I don't like the emotion associated with the first 45 minutes of trading. I make most of my mistakes in that first part of the day, so I usually sit on my hands, read the news, and just watch. Occasionally I might fade a trade, meaning that I would buy if it is down and sell when it's up if I think that early-morning move is way overdone.

Zanger: I use mental stops combined with individual stock action. Most bull markets are "buy the dip" unless the market is going into a nasty correction. If the dip is prompted by a national or global news story, adding on the dip or gap down near the open usually works well.

Ritchie II: This is a bit of a loaded question as I don't think there is any doubt that the current market structure places resting stop orders as a target for market makers to shoot at. So the real question is, what is the best way to avoid being screwed? The answer is to at least try and not place stops that are close to the market, especially in smaller to mid-cap names. If it's a very liquid name, I don't think there's nearly as much an issue.

Lastly, I would strongly advise that mental stops should be used by disciplined professionals *only!* If you have a problem obeying your own stop protocols, then you definitely should not be using mental stops. If you are at the point where adherence to stops is not an issue, only then would I start to lean toward using mental stops.

S8-8: What stop do you use when a stock has broken out but the obvious support is 15–20% below the price? Would a 10% stop give enough room but still be tight enough to control risk?

Minervini: I would hope to be out of a position before a 10% loss; I rarely allow a stock to drop 10%. I don't care where "support" is; I'm never going to risk 15–20% on a trade ever! If support is too far away to use as a stop level, I simply use a percentage stop that I'm comfortable with.

Ryan: On most occasions, I won't buy a stock in that situation because it is too extended. I like to have some technical support, a base, a moving average, a trendline somewhere in the area of my purchase.

Zanger: If I stuck with a 10% stop loss in this situation, I would be broke by now. A 2–3% stop loss is closer to what I actually use. Heck, I often sell stocks that are nowhere near their stops just for acting feebly on their breakouts. They aren't showing the strength I expect from thoroughbreds. Why wait for a stock to roll over and bark like a dog? I say sell the damn thing while it's still up wobbling on that feeble breakout!

Ritchie II: Well, the nature of the question sounds like I would be buying something that is already quite extended, which as I rule I don't do. However, if I were to buy something that doesn't have a very clear stop area that is tight, I would favor a percentage stop based upon my average loss, and I would start with a smaller size than normal, knowing that the odds of my getting stopped are probably higher.

S8-9: What if a stock hits your stop on very anemic volume; do you still cut your loss, or do you hold off and maybe give the stock a bit more room?

Minervini: When the stock price hits my stop, I'm out—period! My goal is to protect my account at a level that makes mathematical sense. The math is the same regardless of volume.

Ryan: Sell. Never give the stock more room. You do that, and you will start rationalizing every loss in your portfolio. Soon your losses will get out of control.

Zanger: It's a situational decision that would depend on what the overall market is doing and things like the normal volatility of the stock itself. At a minimum, I would reduce 30–40% and see what happens.

Ritchie II: If a stock hits a predetermined stop point, I will almost always trim some, although if it's very tight and the stock is pulling in on no volume, I may wait a bit, especially if it's a mid- to smaller-cap name. In general, I try not to ever give stocks more room on the fly and have already decided how much room I'm willing to give a stock beforehand.

S8-10: How do you deal with getting whipped out of trades in a back-and-forth market?

Minervini: If you're getting whipped out excessively, then one of two things is wrong. Either your selection criteria are flawed, or the general market is hostile. You shouldn't have too many whipsaws if you're applying sound principles at the correct time. A whipsaw market is more dangerous than a bear market, because in a bear market you simply get stopped out of everything and go to cash because nothing sets up long.

In a whipsaw market you can suffer what is called "death by a thousand cuts," going in and out, taking many small losses as stocks emerge and then fall back over and over again.

Ryan: The toughest market to deal with is a whipsaw market. Breakouts rarely work, and breakdowns don't work, and so you can get hurt on the long side and the short side. When I see that starting to develop, I cut my exposure down and trade in a much smaller size. I also look to buy more leading stocks during a pulling back and not as many when they are breaking out. The key is to have patience and to wait for the proper setup. Don't force trades when the setups are just not there.

Zanger: As soon as I can discern that the market has started a choppy phase and therefore is lacking a clear trend, I usually stay away from the market entirely. I will wait patiently on the sidelines with my cash for a new trend up. The best advice I can give to new traders is to stay away from choppy markets at all costs. Long or short, chop will eat you alive. Choppy markets can last nine months to a year or more.

Ritchie II: This is actually the toughest kind of environment for my style, especially when the market is sideways or grinding higher but with larger moves back and forth in the general market, because individual stocks can experience larger whipsaws than the general. The answer is pretty simple; if I'm getting whipped around a lot, I trade smaller until things improve.

S8-11: How do you handle a trade if there's an unexpected event? Say you bought at $20 and placed a stop at $19, but the stock gapped down to $15 on news.

Minervini: When my stop is hit, I sell, plain and simple. Otherwise, there is no sense in having a stop in the first place. Slippage is part of trading. But even when I add in slippage, my losses are quite small.

Ryan: If it is unexpected news, sometimes the opening of a gap down is the low and the stock starts to rally higher. I have already suffered a big loss, and I want to give the stock the first 30 minutes to see if there is any chance there was too big an overreaction. If it rallies back more than 50% of the day's drop, I might hold it another day and see if it rallies more. If it goes through the low of the first 30 minutes, then I am out. You just don't want to have a bad loss get worse.

Zanger: On a gap down like this, I usually wait for dip buyers to come in to lift the stock up $1 or $2, and then I start selling until there is nothing left. I move on to the next stock that is setting up and don't give it another thought. A stock experiencing that kind of a gap down is toast. Move on; it doesn't love you anymore, and it moved out with your cat. Get over it and move on!

Ritchie II: Sell!

SECTION NINE

Trade Management

S9-1: Do you ever trade around a core position?

Minervini: Yes. I sometimes will take an oversized position in a stock with a very low-risk entry point, and if the stock moves up quickly, I may take off the excess and nail down a short-term profit. This makes it easier to hold the remaining position, because I already logged a partial profit that serves as a cushion. On the flip side, if I take an oversized position and the trade moves against me, I cut the overweight very quickly. You don't want to be overweight when things are moving against you and underweight when things are working. You want to accomplish just the opposite.

Ryan: I trade around a core position all the time. It's like driving a car: When I see a green light, I step on the gas and initiate or increase my position. If conditions change and I see a yellow light ahead, I might cut back on my position until I see green again. If a stock starts to break down and the light goes red, then I will sell the whole position. You adjust according to how the stock is acting.

Zanger: I typically have one or two massive winners a year. After the stock moves up 20–30%, I shed some stock, and if it pulls back to the 10-day MA or the 21-day MA line, I sometimes like to add back small amounts if I get indications that it's still acting unusually strong. However, I'm more inclined to shed stock on the way up and not add any back. As I mentioned earlier, adding at higher price levels raises my cost basis, and if the stock were to plunge, I would be underwater much more quickly and forced to sell.

Ritchie II: This is something I'm always trying to get better at. Usually I only trade around a position in one of two ways. The first is when the stock hasn't really gotten going yet, where I will often buy and then the stock consolidates; then I will have to reduce it if it doesn't follow through and maybe add it back if it tries to reemerge again. The other situation, and more preferable, is where my profit is at more than two times what I risked and I trade out of some shares; then I look to add back what I sold at a later period if the stock acts well and consolidates again constructively.

S9-2: Can you walk us through a recent winning and losing trade?

Minervini: A trade that worked out pretty nicely was Michaels Companies (MIK); the stock was a recent new issue. I bought it on November 6, 2014, as it emerged from a classic volatility contraction pattern (VCP). The stock closed up 13 out of 16 days; it advanced about 60% in less than four months. I traded out of it earlier, but still made a nice, quick swing profit (see Chart 9.1).

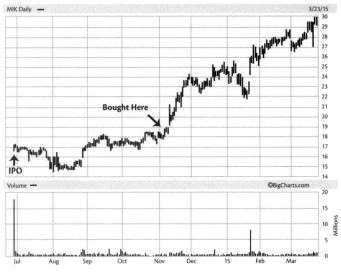

Chart 9.1   **Michaels Companies (MIK), 2014–2015**

An example of an interesting loss is my recent Twitter Inc. (TWTR) trade. I built a position between late March and early April 2015. The stock held up relatively well until April 28 when earnings were supposed to be reported after the close; but instead, earnings leaked out during the day, and the stock started selling off. I had already sold some early in the day and then sold my remaining shares just six minutes before the stock was halted. It then reopened on a gap down of 15%; I only lost 0.16% on the whole trade (see Chart 9.2). The reason why this small loss is so sweet is because I was going to hold into earnings, so the leak actually saved me from what probably would have been a large gap down the next morning.

Chart 9.2   Twitter Inc. (TWTR), 2015

Ryan: Ambarella Inc. (AMBA) is a stock I bought on March 2, 2015, on a nice increase in volume. It broke above all but three days of trading in the base. You can buy a little early when the stock exceeds 90% of the basing area. You don't always wait for the all-time high. The stock had some huge volume the next two days to give it the momentum to continue its move. I then sold out on April 24, 2015, when it started breaking down from a base it had formed over the prior four weeks. I again bought it back on May 15, 2015, but sold it on June 10, 2015, as it looked as if it had gone through a climactic move (see Chart 9.3). The stock moved 40% in a period of three weeks, and that is on top of a 15× move since its IPO price in October 2012.

Chart 9.3   **Ambarella Inc. (AMBA), 2015**

Fiesta Restaurant Group Inc. (FRGI) was a losing trade. I bought the stock trying to emerge out of a base on March 20, 2015. The stock had increasing volume but started to stall. It closed near the low of the day, which is always a bad sign when a stock is trying to break out. I should have paid more attention to the reversal on February 20, 2015, on the biggest volume ever traded in the stock. That was too much to overcome. The stock tried again to move during the next few days, but the demand was not there. I sold on March 25, 2015. The next day it broke the 50-day moving average on tremendous volume, and the stock has been in a downtrend ever since, dropping more than 25% (see Chart 9.4).

Chart 9.4   Fiesta Restaurant Group Inc. (FRGI), 2015

Zanger: Pharmacyclics Inc. (PCYC) was a big runner for a few years. I listed it on my website at $15, and it ran for a few years and got up to $150 and then rested for a good six months. It then proceeded to move out of the six-month base and rip to $168ish, where it rested for two weeks waiting for earnings.

This two-week rest gave this stock a very nice high-level bull flag–like pattern. After earnings, the stock soared $12 and then pulled back into that upper flag-like area. I liked the earnings, and the group was very strong, so I added on the pullback at the $170–$173 area. A few days later the stock started to soar, and it kept racing up and finally got a buyout offer from AbbVie (ABBV) for $258 per share. That was an $80+ gain in just a few weeks (see Chart 9.5).

Chart 9.5   **Pharmacyclics Inc. (PCYC), 2015**

A recent losing trade illustrates how quickly I'm willing to get out a stock if it's not working out as expected. I bought CyberArk (CYBR) as the stock broke a descending channel pattern with increasing volume on June 8, 2015. The price then cleared into new highs but reversed and failed, and I was stopped $1.50 below the buy point (see Chart 9.6).

Ritchie II: One of my better recent winning trades was in Qualys Inc. (QLYS). This was one of my first purchases after coming out of a defensive 100% cash position after the market correction in October 2014. I purchased the stock on October 28, 2014, as it started to move above the $29 level, and it never looked back.

Chart 9.6 **CyberArk Software (CYBR), 2015**

I liked this name because it had held up well during the corrective period in the market and also because it had big earnings and sales and was part of the Internet security group that I was a pretty big fan of. I scaled out of half the trade on November 4, 2014, after a nearly 20% gain, moved my stop to the breakeven, and played the remainder for a much larger move, which I sold on February 10, 2015 (see Chart 9.7).

A recent losing trade was in Lululemon Athletica Inc. (LULU). I bought the stock on February 27, 2015, as it started to break out above the $68 level. But it never really had any follow-through, and I subsequently stopped myself out on March 3, 2015, when the stock took out its previous week's low and closed poorly (see Chart 9.8). Ironically, Goldman

Chart 9.7   **Qualys Inc. (QLYS), 2014–2015**

Chart 9.8   **Lululemon Athletica Inc. (LULU), 2015**

Sachs downgraded the stock three days later—always interesting to observe how the market seemed to know that something like that was coming.

S9-3: What is your trading time frame; how long do you typically hold a momentum stock?

Minervini: On average, my winners are held for two to three
times longer than my losers. My winners can be held for two
or three quarters but rarely for years. The largest part of a big
stock move generally occurs within 12 to 24 months. If you
time the trade right, you can get a pretty good move in short
order. I'm looking to compound my money very rapidly, so
I swing-trade in and out of stocks and rarely hold through
good-size corrections.

Ryan: On winners it would be weeks to months, and for losers
it is days to a few weeks. My best stocks are those that show
an immediate gain, and my biggest winners are the ones I hold
the longest. I want to hold my winners as long as I can. I don't
day-trade. I do much better buying a stock and holding it as
long as the stock is in a nice uptrend. That time period could
be weeks, months, or longer than a year. In today's market,
I'm holding them usually for weeks or months. I never get
locked into a time period. If a stock hits my stop-loss point the
day after I buy it, I will sell it out.

Zanger: Holding times are generally decided by how strong
the overall market is and how fresh or old the bull market
happens to be. I typically hold good strong stocks for no more

than 90 days in a strong bull market and oftentimes for far shorter periods. Losers last one day, possibly two days at a maximum.

Ritchie II: The average hold time varies per trade, but over the last five years my average hold time for losing trades has been only two to three days, and my average hold time for winning trades is between eight and nine trading days. I always take losses very quickly, but I rarely take profits the same way. For me, every trade entry starts as a short-term trade, and then based upon the price action and how well I like the situation will often determine how long I will look to hold a position. If a stock breaks out big right away, I'm more apt to try and play the stock for a much larger move because the best situations always seem to have a way of putting me at a profit right away.

S9-4: Will you ever add to your position when it's down?

Minervini: Almost never. The only time I add to a losing position is when I'm building my position on a pullback, and even then, I add on the way back up and only if the stock is very close to my original purchase price. I never buy more of a stock that is showing me a big loss.

Ryan: I never add to a position where I have a loss. I have already made a mistake; why compound it by adding more to the position? I cannot stand losing positions in my portfolio. They're like a cancer; the losses have to be cut out and not added to. The equity in your portfolio has to be constantly rotated from the losers to the winners.

Zanger: I can't say I'll add to any position when the stock is down, since it might go lower still. It's just not something I do. In fact, I am more likely to reduce when a stock is down. I look for strength, not weakness, to purchase.

Ritchie II: I never average down on a stock.

S9-5: How much above your entry price does a stock have to advance in order to be considered extended such that you will no longer add to it?

Minervini: Once it's a few percentage points beyond the buy point, I leave it alone. I'm looking to get my position on right at the correct buy point. I don't chase stocks.

Ryan: If you are in a strong bull market, I will buy up to 10% from its original buy point. If it is a weak market and you aren't getting much follow-through, 5% would be my limit.

Zanger: If a stock is up 20% or more from its recent base breakout, I would not consider adding more shares no matter what the enticements. The odds don't favor you there like they do from the base breakout.

Ritchie II: It depends more upon what the stock looks like technically; but usually if a stock is up more than 5% beyond its breakout, I won't add unless there's a consolidation period.

S9-6: If you have a large gain in a stock, but it sets up again, would you buy more?

Minervini: Yes, but usually in a smaller amount than my previous purchase. I don't want to run up my average cost.

Ryan: Yes, the big money is made when a stock makes multiple moves during a year or two and has a number of bases along the way.

Zanger: If I have a large gain in a stock, I would've sold out way before it sets up again. However, on the second breakout I would probably buy less since the stock is more expensive from the previous run. The first breakout is usually the best, as institutions didn't have enough shares on the first breakout and were the driving force behind a lot of the demand that pushed the stock up.

Ritchie II: If I'm riding a stock for a bigger move, I will definitely buy more if it sets up, but usually I trade around a core position that I want to hold. For example, say I think a stock could move up 30–50%, but it rips 15–20% in just a few days; I may trade out of some of it, and if the stock consolidates or pulls back in an orderly way, I'll add shares back to it. I usually don't hold my entire position for a big move and then add a lot more at higher prices.

S9-7: Do you ever buy put options (puts) as a hedge to protect or lock in a large gain that you don't want to sell for tax reasons, or if you're only expecting a modest market pullback?

Minervini: Almost never. I occasionally will buy an ETF to short the market in an effort to hedge if I have many names in my portfolio and want to avoid selling down a bunch of stocks to reduce my exposure across the board. But I prefer to stay concentrated in only a handful of names, which allows me to move in and out and change my exposure quickly without having to complicate the equation.

Ryan: Rarely. I try to keep things simple. I buy, sell, short, and cover stocks. Occasionally I buy options.

Zanger: Since I'm a "mark-to-market" trader per IRS rules, my account is tabulated on all gains or losses on December 31 of each year, so hedging for tax reasons at the end of the year does me no good. And since I'm a short-term trader overall, I never hold a stock long enough to qualify for capital gains taxes versus ordinary gains. Therefore, I never hedge for tax purposes, and I never hedge on a market pullback.

Ritchie II: For starters, I don't make trading decisions based upon "tax reasons," as I think it doesn't make sense to let potential tax implications influence shorter-term trading decisions. In regard to put options specifically, I don't buy them as a hedge against longs; if I'm nervous about being too long or having a gain that is extended, I will just trim the underlying position to the point that I no longer feel uneasy about it.

S9-8: When you've reached a desired profit, do you scale out with trailing stops?

Minervini: When I'm at a decent profit, I usually sell into strength before the stock has a chance to move against me and hits my stop on weakness. My "sell half rule" is a win-win solution. If you get indecisive about whether or not to hold a position, a psychological win-win is to sell half; if the stock goes higher, you can say thank God I held half. If the stock goes down, you can say thank God I sold half. Either direction the stock goes, you're correct. If I really like a stock, I sometimes will sell half and move my stop to the breakeven point. This allows me to essentially "free-roll" the second half.

Ryan: It depends on what the move up looked like. If the stock had a fast move up, I might sell some into strength and then move up my stop on the rest of the position. If it has been a steady uptrend and I have been moving up my stop as the stock rises, I would sell it all at once when the stock hits my stop.

Zanger: I don't use trailing stops, as I usually sell into strength on up days, and I hope I'm completely out or have greatly reduced my position before it's topped out. If I'm not completely out, I might then use a break of some moving average line like the 21-day MA line to sell out the last of my position. When trading large positions or thinly traded stocks, it's far easier to reduce into volume spikes after the stock has made a substantial run than to sell on down days with or without volume.

Ritchie II: I do scale out but not with trailing stops. I don't use traditional trailing stops where a stop is resting below the market, but I may set a level in my head whereby I will cut part of the position if it starts giving up too much ground. Ideally I scale out into strength.

S9-9: Should you use trailing stops if you are unable to monitor the markets full-time?

Minervini: Yes, you could do that. But try not to choke off the trade early on. Once you're at a decent profit, then it could be time to cinch up your stop. On parabolic moves, I tighten my stops considerably because pullbacks tend to be larger the steeper the stock moves up.

Ryan: You should check your stocks every day or every other day to move your stops up if need be. I have never had a percentage trailing stop on a stock, but I do use moving averages, trendlines, and volume to place my stops. With today's technology, you can easily check your stops on your phone and change them if you want.

Zanger: Setting mechanical stops with the rest of the herd usually entices the market makers to drop the stock with some artificial price noise and grab that stock at the cheaper price where we clustered our stops. I tried mechanical stops once in the early 1990s, but once I saw how easy it was for someone to grab stock from me at a discount, I never did that again. I think it's absolutely necessary that you keep eyes on your stock at all times and know what the market is doing overall to judge the best exits. Again, I would use a break of one of the areas that I noted as a stop but never a preset stop on a trading platform that bypasses my read of the current market.

Ritchie II: This is really a function of your plan and how concentrated you are. If you are in fairly concentrated positions, then I think you have to have some form of stop protection in the market to keep you from potentially having large losses. Now one could probably argue that your concentration level in your portfolio should be commensurate with the concentration level you have with the actual market, so the less attention you pay, the less concentrated you should be. In the case of smaller positions, I don't think you have to have stops necessarily resting, although I would at least want some form of intraday alert sent to your e-mail or phone that you could potentially act upon.

S9-10: Do you ever adjust your stops once your stock is close to reaching your profit target—i.e., do you adjust your stop to break even or keep the original level?

Minervini: I'm always working to improve my stop while trying not to choke off the trade prematurely. If a stock moves up significantly, I will definitely move my stop to at least my breakeven point. I'm never going to let a big gain turn into a loss. My process is to protect my gain once the stock advances a multiple of my risk or above my average gain. I don't usually move my stop to the breakeven point until the price advances to a multiple of my risk or above my historical average gain.

Ryan: I only adjust the stop in the direction of the trade. So if the stock has had a move of more than 5%, I sometimes move the stop up to the breakeven point or at least closer to it than where I had it on my original purchase. I never move a stop that would increase the amount of loss that I might take from my original purchase.

Zanger: I don't usually have a preset goal, but as the stock progresses up, I reduce in stages. If a stock has run for a few months, I typically would have reduced my position by at least 50% within that time and would be out completely before earnings were announced.

Ritchie II: I don't usually have a predetermined target for a stock; however, I usually don't want to take profits less than my average win, at least into strength. So in that regard, if the stock is past my average win, then I will move the stop to the breakeven point, as my philosophy and trading plan dictate that I don't want to let a better-than-average winner turn into a loss.

S9-11: Do you set price targets on your trades, taking some off the table when the stock reaches that target, or are you more apt to only sell when the chart tells you to?

Minervini: I rarely set targets. I watch the chart and also how much I'm up versus how much I risked. I buy when I think the potential reward outweighs my risk, and I sell when I think the downside risk outweighs the reward. I may sell if I achieve a multiple of my risk, usually somewhere between two and six times my stop loss; at that point I follow the stock up with a backstop.

Ryan: I am more apt to sell when the chart starts breaking support points. The problem about setting price targets is that the best stocks usually end up going a lot further than anyone expects. That 20% profit you took might feel good at the time but then become very painful when that stock moves up 300%. However, a lot depends on how quickly a stock makes that first move, how big the earnings are, and what the general market is doing.

Zanger: The real problem with price targets is that if you set a target of $80 and the stock runs to $120, you've missed a large move. I have set targets in the past and likely will do so again in the future, but the stock action trumps targets for me. Targets are typically predicated on historical or statistical behavior, which is more or less average behavior. The real winners where you make the big money are far from average. Targets are like shooting a winning horse at the starting gate.

Ritchie II: In regard to selling into strength, my minimum target would be above my average gain, which is usually two times my risk or more. But I don't usually set arbitrary targets for taking profits, as I like to see the price action and how it's acting relative to other stocks in my portfolio or on my watch list.

S9-12: Do you ever sell a weak-acting stock before it hits your stop? What factors would cause you to sell early?

Minervini: I have a list of "violations" that I look for right after I buy a stock. If the stock breaks out on low volume and comes back in on heavy volume, that's a violation. Three or four lower lows with no supportive action are a violation. A close below the 20-day moving average or worse the 50-day line right after a breakout is another violation. Lack of follow-through and more down days than up days are violations. If these violations start piling up, I may sell the stock even before my stop is hit.

Ryan: Yes, I sometimes sell before the price hits my stop because of a number of factors. General market averages could be rolling over, or a stock within its group is indicating conditions are changing. It might even be that the relative strength of the stock has been dropping and I have better-acting stocks that I could move money to. I want to give a stock time to make a move but don't want my capital to be sitting in something that is going sideways for too long. General market weakness is usually the main reason, but it could be group weakness or just too many stocks blowing up when earnings have been reported.

Zanger: A market break is one of the more significant ones. Having the stock stall out or cross below one of my moving average lines or an elevated trendline could trigger an exit as well. I sell weak stocks as soon as I determine that they are weakening. Weak stocks tend to roll over fast and tie up your cash, preventing you from acquiring better-moving stocks. I've learned it's best either to sell out of them right away and move into others that are acting far better or to stay in cash.

Ritchie II: Yes, if a stock breaks out and just stalls with no follow-through and I want to add another name but don't want to add more total exposure to my portfolio, I will sometimes cut one stock to buy another. Also, if the stock doesn't do what I expected—which is to break out and go quickly, but it just sits—I may cut it out, knowing that I can buy it back if it breaks out again.

Let's say I am in five positions, I've been stopped on three or four of them, the general market is acting very poorly, and I'm seeing distribution in the major averages, plus other stocks on my watch list are acting poorly. I may make the decision to just move to cash and sell out any remaining holdings I have before they hit their predetermined stops.

S9-13: Do you ever sell a stock simply because you realized you made a mistake and made a poor buy decision?

Minervini: Absolutely! The minute you realize you've made a mistake, correct it. I'm looking to compound money, not mistakes. Holding when you know you've made a mistake is illogical.

Ryan: Yes, one of the most important traits an investor can have is the ability to admit a mistake and take as small a loss as possible. Big egos in the market lead to big losses. To fight with the market and not be flexible enough to admit to a mistake will just lead to serious losses. Most doctors make bad investors because they can rarely admit to a mistake, because in their profession admitting a mistake would probably get them sued.

Zanger: Absolutely, and the faster I sell that piece of junk and move on to a great mover, the better I'll sleep.

Ritchie II: I can't think of a time when I've done that, but I certainly would get out immediately if I made a really foolish purchase.

S9-14: How do you decide when to sell a winning stock that is up substantially and starts to pull back, especially if the market uptrend is intact?

Minervini: There isn't a fixed percentage. My basic rule of thumb is to never let a decent profit turn into a loss. If the stock has not moved up much, I stick with my original stop. But once I've attained a good-size profit, I go into profit protection mode. Once I'm at a decent gain, I protect it by backstopping a good part of the gain. I would hope that I'd already sold some into strength, which is my preferred method.

Ryan: It is usually not a percentage pullback that I am looking to sell but some technical or fundamental change that takes place. I don't usually make all-or-nothing decisions, especially on winning positions, but instead I scale in and out of them. If something has had a big move and is extended and looks like it is starting to pull back, I might sell a portion of the position, but I never want to lose a position in a stock that looks like a leader. Once you sell out the entire position, sometimes you can miss the next move higher.

Zanger: That really depends on many factors. What percentage of my portfolio is comprised of that stock? How steep is the angle of ascent on the chart, how far has the stock run, and how liquid is it? The steeper the angle of ascent and the more it has become extended from the breakout area, the less room I give it. For example, if the stock is moving up at a 30 degree angle of ascent and it consumes a modest percentage of my portfolio, I'm likely to give it much more room. And yes, implied in that statement is my observation that charts showing steeper ascent are more volatile.

Many traders use a break of the 10-day simple moving average (SMA) line, which I use occasionally, or the 21-day SMA line as a sell point. Both are effective and are used often by me and others. I can also use an elevated rising trendline or a key reversal bar. I never hold myself to a single tool; my toolbox is open at all times, and I use the right tool that fits the situation.

Ritchie II: This is one of the harder parts of swing trading in my opinion, because often the stocks you take the biggest profits on wind up going much higher. The answer lies more in the amount of what I call "normal" action you're willing to stomach. For example, if a stock runs up substantially with no pullbacks, then a larger pullback would be normal. If you don't want to sit through it, then you have to trim your position to a level that you're willing to hold through.

Ideally I look more at volume on the pullback than a strict percentage, but if a stock has had, say, more than a 20% move with no pullback, then it should not give back more than, say, two-thirds of the move, and the harder it pulls in, the more I'm going to want to see it bounce back right away. The price action should always be confirming to the upside and ideally with volume regardless of how much it pulls in. If a stock pulls in on above-average volume and just sits there, then that's a sign that it's at least not being currently accumulated.

S9-15: How do you handle the thin line between taking profits into strength and letting your winners run?

Minervini: I don't concern myself with getting the high, which is rarely possible; I sell when I think the risk-reward proposition has changed from positive to negative. At the beginning of a new bull market, I'm more likely to let a winner run. But I typically trade out of anywhere between one-third and one-half to as much as 75 percent of a position on a swing trade and then hold the remaining shares for a bigger move. With a new market leader, I will often use the 50-day line as a trailing sell point.

Ryan: That is a judgment call based on how strong the stock has been. If it has just had a climactic move of 30% in a matter of three weeks after it has already had a move for over a year, I would definitely start selling. If it is the first move coming out of a long base, then I would continue to hold it.

Zanger: It's all about price behavior for me. Stocks can run quickly for a week or two and then fall like a brick while others continue to run months more. I think it's best to reduce into fast movers until you find your win-win situation. By this, I mean if the stock runs up and I sell 50% of my position and then the stock comes back down to my original buy area, I can sell the rest and still walk away with a tidy gain. On the other hand, if I take 50% off after a sharp run and the stock continues to run, I'm still winning with the remaining 50%.

Ritchie II: I try and find harmony in both. Here I think knowing and having a reasonable expectation based upon your trading metrics is essential. Every kind of position trader that is trying to make more on his or her respective gains has to let the winners ride to a degree, but how far and for how long is the real question. The key is to let the winners run relative to their losses so that the net expectancy is positive. If you are taking very small losses, you may only have to let gains ride a couple of days, and you can still sell a good majority of them into strength; don't get wrapped up in the idea of having to catch an entire move in order to be successful. You just have to catch enough of a move so that it can more than offset your average loss expectations, and you ought to be able to do that often by selling into strength.

S9-16: Is there a time to hold a stock for a large move versus to trade out and take a swing profit?

Minervini: First, you should define your trading style; are you a trader or investor? You can trade around positions, but if you don't decide on a style, you're going to drive yourself nuts. When a stock goes higher, you will kick yourself for not holding; and when you hold and it goes lower, you will be wishing you had sold. The key is to make a decent gain and to keep your losses smaller than your winners. During the beginning stages of a new bull market is the best time to hold, and in the late stages of a bull market—usually after several years—is the best time to trade shorter-term moves and sell into strength.

Ryan: If you are at the start of a new bull market and you have some leading stocks in your portfolio, you should hold for the longer move. If a stock has been moving for a long time and has had numerous bases, then you might want to think about just trading that move.

Zanger: When the Fed starts to reduce interest rates, I'm more likely to let stocks run for a longer period of time. Unless of course, we are in a major meltdown like 2001, where the Fed started to lower rates after a massive bubble and stocks still plunged. The Nasdaq gave up 80% of its value. Naturally I would have adjusted the strategy accordingly.

Ritchie II: This is something I'm continuing to try and improve upon, but in general there are situations where I try and do this, and this is one of the main reasons I try not to have static targets on anything I buy upon entry. The first thing I want to see is how the stock acts when I buy it. Some of the best trades tend to put me under little to no pressure almost immediately; if the timing is perfect, they may never even trade below my entry price. That is the first and most important reason to potentially hold for a bigger gain. Other factors would include what type of technical pattern it's coming out of, how big the stock is in terms of market cap, how well it's followed, what its earnings and sales are, and what group it's in.

S9-17: Do you ever use a time stop?

Minervini: My time stops are generally based on my initial entry and what I expect to happen. For example, if the 6:05

train that you take to work each morning has not arrived in the station and it's now 7:45, you can assume that something has probably gone wrong. With my trading, it's based on the difference between my assumption and what actually takes place. Let's just say that I like my trains to come in on schedule. I will often sell a stock simply because it did not do what I expected.

Ryan: No. I judge the movement of a stock relative to other leaders. If it isn't moving higher while other are, its relative strength will drop, and I will eventually sell it out. So I don't have a specific time frame of X amount of days or weeks that I use.

Zanger: That depends on the move of the stock, but I do reduce when the move is long in the tooth, which is similar in concept to a time stop.

Ritchie II: Sometimes the shorter my time frame in trading is, the more I use time stops, so I'm much more likely to use a time stop on a day trade than I will a swing trade. As I widen my time horizon, I tend to stick to price stops.

S9-18: How do you handle positions heading into their earnings? Do you hold the stock through earnings, reduce your position, sell outright, or hold on and if it gaps below your stop, just sell ASAP?

Minervini: Sometimes I hold, and sometimes I don't. It's not an exact science. If I don't have a profit cushion, I will often reduce my shares, especially if the position is oversized; I never hold a large position into earnings. If the stock breaks down on a poor report, I almost always sell immediately. I don't care if later it comes back and, in hindsight, it turns out I was wrong to sell. At that moment, I'm already wrong, and I'm not interested in protecting my ego; my only concern is to protect my portfolio from additional loss. You could use options to limit your risk or hedge the position, not something I generally do. My rule is to never hold a large position going into an important event, like earnings.

Ryan: If I don't own it, I won't buy it before earnings. If I have a nice profit, I will probably reduce the size of the position. Sometimes I might even buy some puts as protection but not too often. If it gaps down below my stop, I will see if there is any rally in the first 30 minutes. If it goes below the low of the first 30 minutes, it will be gone.

I will hold through earnings if I have a profit cushion already built into the stock. I also have to know a lot more about the company's fundamentals before the report. I never like to take a new position in a stock right before earnings. Sometimes I reduce the size of the position, especially if the stock has been running up into earnings. The run-up might suggest that expectations for the company to beat its earnings estimates are too high.

Zanger: As I noted above, I never hold through earnings. I sell all positions the day before earnings and then reconsider the stock should it move up on good earnings news and strong forward guidance. This is predicated on the stock coming out of a well-formed base on its chart. While I may miss some great movers to the upside right at the onset, there is nothing sweeter than avoiding the stock that just gapped down $20 to $80 on an earnings miss. The risk of holding through earnings and living with the financial and emotional damage is rarely justified by the occasional gains. In fact, I sell a full day before earnings just in case earnings are released early by mistake.

Ritchie II: I never hold a large position or hold a loser. I have a checklist of sorts that I run through, but the most important thing I want is to not have a large position and then to see that I'm at a profit in the trade already; if I don't have a profit, I almost never hold, unless the position at that point is very small. If it gaps well below my stop, I usually just sell; if it gaps close to a key area or just below it, I may wait a little bit to see if it gets any support, but usually I'm looking then to sell into any bounce I get.

S9-19: Do you sell existing positions if you are fully invested and a new stock sets up? If yes, which ones do you sell first— the ones with the highest gains or the weakest performers?

Minervini: I may sell an extended stock to buy a fresh new breakout. But you have to be careful not to sell out strong stocks just because they are short-term extended; often the strongest stocks are the ones that go even much higher. Most of the time—in the strongest names—I will hold some shares to play a larger move. If I have losses, I will usually sell my losers first. If they hit my stops, then I have fresh cash automatically.

Ryan: The weaker performers are always the first to go. You have to have some patience and give a stock time to make a move. If it continues to go sideways while the rest of the market is in an uptrend, eventually its relative strength against all the other stocks in the market is going to fall off, and the stock should be sold. You want the equity in your portfolio always rotating to the stocks that are starting to move higher.

Zanger: There are times when I might reduce a stock that has had a nice run and is now extended. Or I might cut completely out of a laggard and then try a newly identified stock and see how it runs. Obviously the weakest-performing stock would be my first choice to cut.

Ritchie II: I will do this sometimes, but only if I determine the situation I'm getting into is better than the situation I'm already in. So in that sense, I will never sell a winner to buy a new position. That's illogical to me, because I'm trading out of less risk to buy more, as a new position has the full risk premium attached to it versus a position that I already own that is working for me. Now I may sell a position that is only up fractionally or hasn't really followed through; but I will often have a plan to repurchase that position if it can recover and break back out again.

S9-20: How do you manage big winning positions that run up 20% or more in just a few days or a few weeks?

Minervini: If the stock is really strong, I try to give it extra time. I may sell a portion and then hold the rest. Like I said previously, you have to be careful not to sell out really strong stocks just because they are short-term extended—especially in the beginning of a new bull market, the strongest stocks could be market leaders about to embark on a major advance.

Ryan: I continue to hold them. Stocks that demonstrate that kind of strength are usually the leaders, and you want to try to get a long-term move out of them.

Zanger: Reducing into strength is usually how I manage it. The big problem for many new traders is that they believe this one stock is going to make them rich. They keep adding or hold for much longer than they should. Many of these very fast movers can be exhaustion moves or gaps. In any event, I reduce at the 20% profit area to lock in gains, and I let the rest ride. I hold to the various stop strategies I noted above, such as the 21-day simple moving average line.

Ritchie II: By definition, these are positions I would probably want to hold for a bigger move, but generally I would still scale out of a portion of the position into a run like that, which puts you in a really strong position psychologically because you've taken a really nice profit on a piece; so if it pulls in, you're glad you took some, and if it rallies significantly further, then you're glad that you're still holding the remaining piece.

S9-21: How do you manage the successful trades? What types of sell signals do you use?

Minervini: There are many things to look for that could indicate it's time to step aside from a winning trade. The main thing to realize is that you're virtually never going to get the high price. Nailing highs and lows is not what successful trading is about. The goal is to sell higher than where you bought. The goal is to make more money than you risk and to do it repeatedly.

Once my position turns into a decent profit, I will often move my stop to the breakeven at that point. I'm generally looking to sell into strength while the stock is advancing. I don't like trailing stops, but I often will set a "backstop." That's a stop that protects a certain portion of my gain and then allows the stock to trade as long as it holds above that level. If the stock moves up much from there, then I may either sell it or raise the backstop. As the stock goes higher, I get tighter and tighter with my backstop, eventually choking off the trade and nailing down my profit.

Ryan: Once I have a nice gain and it looks like I am in a leading stock, I give it room to move. The 8% stop loss is used only at the initial purchase price. After that, I move my stop loss to the breakeven. As the stock moves higher, I then use moving averages, trendlines, and areas of consolidation to give me spots where I should protect my profits.

If the stock has made a big move, I look for a change in how the stock is acting. Is the stock dropping on increased volume and rallying on lighter volume? Has it broken down from the last base it was in? Did it break below its 50-day or 200-day moving average or a recent uptrend line? Most of the change I am looking for is technical in nature, and I focus on the stock's behavior.

Zanger: Managing the successful trades means you let them run until you get to a sell signal, such as a break of a very steep rising trendline on volume, or a break of a 21-day MA line, or a break of a 50-day MA line. My preference would be the break of a 21-day MA line or a very steep elevated trendline.

Ritchie II: I don't have a sell signal per se. The first and most important thing is where the stock is relative to how much I originally set out to risk. If I'm at a multiple of my risk, then I'm looking for possible signs to take profits: Does it have a really large up day or a reversal? Those are things I look at sometimes. I'll also look at how far it's extended from a certain moving average. Or if it's accelerating above or near the top of its own uptrend, that is often a sign to take some off.

I will never sell a stock into strength that isn't at least twice as much as my original risk amount; that's based on my longer-term trading metrics. Once a stock is past that point, I use a list of things to determine whether to take part or all of the profits. This list includes how good I perceive the price action to be, how well my overall trading is going, and how strong the earnings and sales are, as well as what group the stock is in.

SECTION TEN

Psychology

S10-1: How do you maintain discipline and fight the urge to overtrade? When do you just sit on your hands?

Minervini: I fight the urge by letting the stocks and my criteria guide me. The urge to trade is not part of my trading plan. I won't trade unless certain criteria are met. As a result, when stocks set up according to my discipline, I trade. When they don't, I sit out. It's that simple, but only if you can divorce yourself from your opinion and let the market guide you.

Ryan: I don't like to lose capital, and when I start to have a number of losses in a row, I just trade smaller and smaller. There are times when you should have no exposure to the market from the long side, within either a bear market or a sideways market.

Zanger: Observe and live in the firestorm of the market for a few dozen years, and you'll learn not to stick your hand in the fire when you see it. I got burned too many times to forget what "chop and slop" truly means, whether long or short. Market behavior follows distinct repetitive patterns that teach clear lessons, so when you see a market starting to act badly, you've learned instinctively that it's time to back off for the required weeks or months. During that time you don't go on vacation and turn your back on the market; you still need to be watching the market every day so you'll know when it has calmed down and is back to normal. Diligence even during a choppy market is part of good timing.

Ritchie II: This is one of the hardest things, especially when you start out if you are trying to make a living, because the need to eat can be very powerful in forcing you to trade. The easiest solution is to closely watch your recent trading results and to quickly adjust the frequency of your trading in accordance with how you're doing. When things are going well, keep taking trades; and when things are not going well, be more selective.

S10-2: What advice can you give to help a trader avoid analysis paralysis and help him or her take decisive action?

Minervini: If you're nervous and finding it difficult to take action and pull the trigger, trade small; trade as small as you need to until you feel comfortable. Over time you will gain confidence, but only if you cut your losses and avoid big drawdowns. Big losses will hurt your bank account as well as your confidence, and that will make you even more apprehensive.

Ryan: You should have a method that narrows down to a precise set of rules. If a stock meets all the criteria you set down, then you go with it; if not, do nothing.

Zanger: I think there are two parts to that "analysis paralysis" question as far as market trading is concerned. First is just being able to pull the trigger on a trade. The second and equally important is allowing your analysis to paralyze you while in a trade that you should exit, just because of the emotional commitment to the analysis.

On the first, if you are trapped overanalyzing whether to enter a trade, then you are more than likely afraid of failure. Trade small positions; use puts and calls; do whatever it takes to get some real cash on the line at modest risk. Confidence builds from success, no matter how small.

On the second circumstance, traders often get frozen thinking their stock is too great to break down or go into a deep correction. They hold steadfast to the belief their stock is in an uptrend, and when it does plunge in a clearly unhealthy manner, they refuse to take action before it plunges further. Or if their stock breaks a high-level moving average such as the 10-day, they hold firm to their faith. The answer to this paralysis is simple: set your line in the sand before entering the trade and make sure you stick to it.

Ritchie II: I think every trader at some point has to have a set of conditions that are "no-brainers" where the trader always takes at least a small position. You make a trading plan that requires you to take a trade when x, y, and z criteria are met. Then, if the no-brainer trade or situation is yielding good results, you build on that by either taking more similar trades or looking to pyramid to the existing position.

S10-3: How do you build the confidence it takes to pull the trigger on large positions?

Minervini: Again, start small. Over time you will gain the confidence to trade larger. Having low confidence in the beginning isn't necessarily a bad thing. If you're overconfident, you may do something very risky and then lose all your confidence from taking large losses. It's better to start out humble and build your confidence one trade at a time.

Ryan: Success always helps build confidence. If you have been picking some good stocks consistently with small positions, then you should gradually start your initial purchase with a larger amount. So if you have been doing well with 5% positions, then start your positions at 7–8%. I only want a position to get to be 15–25% of my portfolio because of market appreciation or because I have added to the position as it has built subsequent bases.

Zanger: Years of seeing what works and what doesn't. You learn to read earnings properly and identify stocks that dominate their space. Combine that with an eye for chart patterns and solid bases along with the overall market behavior, and you will have plenty of confidence for the big trades.

Ritchie II: Success. This is where having a string of winners or even a string of good market actions gives you the confidence to take bigger-size trades because you've financed the additional risk with your last few winning trades. Most home run hitters don't swing for the fences, but they often find that home runs come when they're just making good solid contact consistently with the ball. Stock trading is no different from anything else; you get a little bit of success, and that gives you the added confidence to start swinging a little harder—or bigger in this case.

S10-4: What do you do when you have a series of losses; what adjustments do you make to your trading?

Minervini: I trade smaller. The more I lose, the smaller I trade. If I take a series of losses in a row, it usually means general market conditions aren't right.

Ryan: I trade smaller and smaller. I slow down and try not to quickly make back the equity I just lost in one trade. At times I might even stop for a number of days or weeks and take a break. I go over my rules and review what has worked in the past. I also do some self-examination to see if I can be focused enough to succeed at that time. You could be going through some events in your life where you should stop trading until you can clearly focus again.

Zanger: If I have a series of losses, then the market is misbehaving, and it's time to stand back and wait for the market to start behaving properly again. This could be a few weeks to a few months or longer. A few years would not even be out of the question, as was the case from March 2000 to March 2003 when the Nasdaq lost 80% of its value.

Ritchie II: If I have no gains to speak of or don't have any open gains, then I will start reducing risk by taking either fewer trades or smaller size. If I buy four stocks and I get stopped out of two of them, but the other two are paying for the losses, then I stay the course, although I may temper the next few buys to see where things shake out.

S10-5: You seem to be using the same strategy for many years—how have you avoided style drift?

Minervini: Commitment. You have to commit to a strategy. Your relationship with your stock strategy is like a marriage; how good a marriage do you think you would have if you cheated on your spouse and weren't totally committed? Find a system that makes sense to you—something that you believe in—and commit to it. Understand that success is not going to happen overnight. It takes time, and it takes commitment.

Ryan: I have tried other approaches, but I haven't found one yet that does as well as a growth stock approach. Not that there aren't other approaches or strategies that do well, but this seems to suit my personality the best.

Zanger: You have to adjust to current market conditions, but momentum trading really doesn't change. It's the difference between strategy and tactics. My tactics change, but my strategy doesn't.

One always has to adjust to the current market behavior despite the invariant outcome of the market, which is to serve up all the same chart patterns over and over again. Some tactical changes a trader must address in adapting to current market conditions are reflected in the questions, Is the market simply drifting higher, or is it roaring higher? Is it a sluggish market, and do breakouts commonly fail? And one of the most important tactical variations of all is not being on margin or in options when the market goes into a correction. I'm a momentum trader who adapts his style to what the market throws at him.

Ritchie II: This question doesn't apply to me as much, as I've always taken somewhat of a multistrategy approach where I trade a portfolio of equities on a shorter-term time frame, namely from two days to two months. Within the portfolio, I will use the excess cash (my average percentage invested per day is very low) to do some shorter-term trading in very liquid futures.

S10-6: Are there ever times that you deviate from your discipline? What caused you to lose your focus? How did you get back on track?

Minervini: I'm human and certainly not perfect, so yes. However, if I do deviate, it's not by much, and I get back on track pretty quickly. It wasn't always that way. When I first started trading, I deviated all the time. Of course, the consistency of my results was in line with the consistency of my discipline. I finally took a real hard look at what I was doing and decided once and for all that I would stick to a plan and learn from my mistakes, analyzing them so closely and understanding them so intimately that I would not re-create them.

Lots of things can tempt you to lose focus. That's why it's so important that you have a set of rules and a plan to guide you. This way, when you're faced with a tough decision, you won't have much to think about; you just follow your plan. I'm flexible with my observations but not with my philosophy. Techniques and tactics evolve, but fundamental truths remain constant.

Ryan: I have tried quite a few other approaches. For instance, I have tried buying turnaround situations, buying on pullbacks, buying on Fibonacci retracements, and a number of other strategies. I have never really deviated from the basic high-growth stock approach I've used since working at William O'Neil & Co., but I have tried to incorporate some of these strategies into a portion of my portfolio. I have always found that I would have the greatest success when I would buy companies with accelerating earnings breaking out to new highs. It is what worked in the past and what will continue to work into the future.

Zanger: I think most chart-reading momentum traders will deviate from their master plan at some point and try new things. If you assume the learning process never ends in the trading game, then this is no surprise. Personally, I think boredom has been at the root of many of my trading mistakes.

This begets the larger question, when does healthy experimentation apart from one's trading discipline cross the line to something else? It's easy to get caught up in your own thoughts and perceptions, divorced from reality. Well, the market has a quick cure; it knocks you out cold on the canvas and puts the smelling salts right under your nose. I'm kidding a bit, but there is nothing better than getting smacked on a few trades to bring you back to reality and the crystal clarity of what is happening with you and the market.

Ritchie II: I never deviate from discipline when it comes to taking losses, which is automatic. For me, to deviate is more in taking trades that are wider and looser, meaning using criteria that might not be as solid as they should be or trading something that is a bit outside my area of competence. For me, this tends to happen in two varieties: Either I'm on a really good streak and feeling like I can do no wrong, so I start shooting at things I ordinarily wouldn't. Or I have nothing that meets my strictest of criteria, so I start forcing a trade here and there. I get back on track usually by losing and then being forced to refocus on what I do best.

S10-7: Would you prefer to have only a few big winners even if it means having many more small losers; or is it more important to have many winners to keep your mindset positive?

Minervini: I like to build in failure and try to keep my approach profitable even at a low percentage of profitable trades or low batting average. I would rather take more small losses. I prefer to control my edge through managing the losses in relation to my gains as opposed to trying to control the percentage of profitable trades, which you have no direct control over.

Ryan: No. I have always said that if you have two or three really good stocks a year, it makes up for all the small losses and much more.

Zanger: My biggest gains have come from just a few dozen massive movers over the past 20 years. Everything else is statistically insignificant if you weigh this purely on a profit basis. I would add, though, that I routinely have more losers in a year than winners since I test the water all the time with very small positions. These tests are actually necessary to help me avoid boredom in between big moves. And admittedly, testing the waters has helped me find a few of those better-moving stocks as well. It goes without saying, of course, that I keep very tight stops on those stocks that fail to move up or that undercut the pivot area.

Ritchie II: Ideally I would like to have lots of smaller gains so I can turn the edge over faster; however, as my size grows, it does become more challenging. So I'm always looking for select situations where I can ride a bigger move as well.

S10-8: How do you know when your strategy may be broken versus just being out of favor with the current market?

Minervini: I'm using timeless principles that should never be permanently broken unless the law of supply and demand suddenly doesn't apply. That would be like the law of gravity changing. Not very likely. There are certainly periods when trading is challenging regardless of which strategy you use, and at some point every strategy underperforms. During those periods, I focus on not losing much and readying myself for when the strategy gets back in favor.

Ryan: My strategy has never been broken. It is what works in the stock market. There are times when value may be in favor and outperform growth stocks, but that doesn't mean my strategy is broken. Eventually, the market always comes back to where the earnings are growing.

Zanger: When stocks continually fail their breakouts, I know momentum trading won't work for me. A market correction or sloppy behavior has obviously started, so it's time to step aside for a few months or more and wait for a trend.

Ritchie II: Answering this dilemma is often the difference between weathering a drawdown and throwing in the towel. The way I have handled it thus far is by trying to have a realistic understanding of my trading and how probability theory can adversely affect me. So if I have a set of trading results over a given period that I'm confident are statistically relevant, then I can run a series of simulations to see what my worst projected drawdowns could potentially be at a given mathematical edge. If I experience a drawdown worse than probability theory says is possible or *way* outside of statistical norms, then it would tell me my initial assumption on the strength of my edge is highly suspect.

This can get complicated, but the real point here is that no one gives up at new equity highs, so you have to have realistic assumptions for what drawdowns are normal versus the ones that are telling you something is wrong in the bigger picture with either you or your approach.

S10-9: Each of you experienced losses before everything came together and you became profitable. What was your mindset to stay so positive or have such a strong belief that

your method would eventually work, especially back in the day when there wasn't as much ability to learn from others to see that there is a way to beat the markets?

Minervini: That's precisely why my approach is based on timeless truths. I remove one of the important question marks, or what I call the "strategy factor." This narrows it down to the most important variable, me. I always took responsibility for my results and never blamed outside factors. If you can be objective and learn from your mistakes, eventually you will acquire the correct knowledge. Then it's a matter of being disciplined.

But you have to believe in your own ability, and you must make a commitment. Forget about the clock. Becoming great at anything worthwhile takes time, and that amount of time differs from person to person. If you don't get the hang of it in one year, then give it two years; and if you don't get it in two years, give it three, and so on. When you set a deadline and say, "If I don't get it by X amount of time," you've already sealed your fate. Life rewards those who make an unconditional commitment. Bottom line: There are many ways to skin the market. But ultimately, it's not the gun; it's the gunner.

Ryan: I was fortunate to watch Bill O'Neil and how he operated in the market, and so I had an example of success. When I experienced losses, I knew that with a lot of hard work to figure out where I was making my mistakes, I could turn my performance around. Once I corrected my mistakes, I became extremely focused on buying only one type of setup. I didn't care about any other method or setup. That is when my returns just took off.

Zanger: I was so tired of working 80 to 90 hours a week building swimming pools for the wealthy in Beverly Hills and not making more than $60,000 per year. I always knew the big money was to be made in stocks or real estate, and I was going to get out of building pools if it was the last thing I did. I opted for the stock market. I assumed I could start with as little as 15 grand, and if I went on margin, I would have $30,000 as my starting base to trade. If I could double that in six months, I would have $60,000; then if I could double it again in another six months, I would have $120,000, and so on. The overly optimistic math presented a clear path out of the pool-building business because I was going to get out no matter what it took.

I got my first view of chart patterns and their power watching a show on KWHY-TV on UHF channel 22 in the late 1970s and early 1980s. A fellow named Gene Morgan came on 30 minutes after the market close with a show called *Charting the Market.* He used an easel and Xeroxed copies of charts from the book known then as *Daily Graphs.* He would put the Xeroxes on the easel and mark up chart patterns, explaining how they foretold the future price movement of stocks. He used to show historical charts with flags and pennants, cups and handles, and parabolic curves.

I thought these were wild concepts, and I started going to some of his free seminars. Unfortunately, all he wanted to do was sell interests in oil and gas ventures. So, on my own,

I started going down to the offices where *Daily Graphs* was printed in Los Angeles and buying the printed books every Saturday morning. I spent all my free time looking at close to 2,000 stocks in these books, trying to discern the chart patterns that Gene showed on TV. I could not find a single chart pattern if my life depended on it. Of course, what I realized was unless someone pointed them out for me, I could not interpret the chart patterns properly. I hadn't spent nearly enough time on chart pattern recognition.

Daily Graphs recommended a book called *How to Make Money in Stocks* by William O'Neil along with *Encyclopedia of Chart Patterns*. I jumped in with both feet and broadened my reading to include Jesse Livermore's book *Reminiscences of a Stock Operator*. Things started to gel for me. It took a few years of reading these books repeatedly and applying what I was seeing on my AIQ charting program to real-time trading during the day before I got the hang of it.

Ritchie II: I certainly didn't have confidence initially that what I was doing was going to work. In fact, some of what I was doing wasn't working, but I did have confidence that if I managed risk and compounded upon ideas that did work, I would have a chance at making it. My first year I hardly made anything. I did have one strategy that returned a large amount in my portfolio, but it had the smallest allocation, so I knew if I just allocated more to what was working, I would have done better. So while the bottom line hadn't grown massively, I felt my knowledge and experience had, such that to quit at that point would have seemed more foolish than to continue.

S10-10: Do you conduct post-analysis? If yes, can you explain the process and how you use that information to improve your trading?

Minervini: Yes, I'm a big fan of post-analysis; it's what turned my trading around early in my career. I even created a software tool that I use, and also provide to our Private Access members, to measure trading results, which includes a unique proprietary distribution curve. In addition, I conduct a very straightforward evaluation, which is to simply mark on a chart where I bought and sold and then study the results looking for common denominators. This basic analysis can be a real eye-opener. The key is to develop a feedback loop and stay in touch with your trading results regularly. Then it's a matter of letting what you've learned make its way back into your trading.

Ryan: When I buy a stock, either I print out the chart with the statistical information that is most important, or I take a screenshot of the information and put it in a file to review it after I sell the stock. I also make notes about why I bought the stock and what the condition of the current market environment was. From those actual purchases and sales, I then study where I was right and where I made mistakes. You can learn more from studying your own investing and trading patterns than just about anything else.

Zanger: I do conduct post-analysis every now and then, but when I was starting out, I used to carry around a yellow pad of paper and write down all my mistakes. That's ultimately how I created my 10 Golden Rules and Trading Tips that I have on my website, and I still use them today.

Ritchie II: Tracking my trades is something I always do. Every trade I make gets tracked within its appropriate strategy, so I have accurate trading metrics for everything I'm doing. Then I can make better assumptions about possible drawdowns within a given approach or my overall portfolio. I'm amazed at the number of people who fail to do this. I'm not saying it's essential in order to succeed, but it is for me.

I believe that if struggling traders spent as much time studying their trades as they did their charts, then they would be way better off. Your actual trading results have a wealth of information about you even if your trading is unprofitable. Most losing traders don't do it because it's painful to look their poor results in the eye. The best thing to do is study your results for patterns of what you do well and where you struggle. If you can find some obvious areas to improve, then you can increase or decrease your exposure accordingly. However, if you don't track your trades, then you will never know the truth about your trading or yourself as a trader.

SECTION ELEVEN

Final Thoughts

S11-1: What were your hardest obstacles to overcome to become a successful trader?

Minervini: In the beginning, the hardest thing was to maintain discipline religiously; which meant to stop having "just-this-one-time" moments. You know, when the stock chart says sell, sell, sell! but you say "just this one time" I'm going to hold on and give it some extra room.

Early on in my career, I would cut my losses most of the time, but every now and then I would hold on for dear life, and those few large losses would wreak havoc. I also had to learn to practice patience. The fear of missing out is a strong emotion when trading. It is the root of many trading failures. I have two main rules: (1) no forced trades. (2) no big losses. You must develop "sit-out power," the ability to wait for correct setups and not force action and take subpar trades. Then it's a matter of developing the discipline to cut your losses quickly in those situations that don't work out as you expected.

Ryan: Adapting a new way of thinking is the hardest obstacle to overcome. You have to be able to admit mistakes and correct those mistakes. That is very tough because that takes self-examination, analyzing what you have done incorrectly in the past. Most people just don't want to do that. When I looked at mistakes I was committing early on in my career, I found that I was buying too many stocks that were extended from their breakout point. Once I corrected that mistake, my performance took off. I also had to get used to buying stocks hitting new highs. At first, that was very scary to do, but as I got used to it, it became very natural.

Zanger: Learning to properly read charts was the greatest obstacle by far, and not appreciating or respecting the power of a steep market correction, as well as a market break when on margin.

Ritchie II: The hardest obstacle in trading is getting "over the hump." This to me is when you have a methodology that works in the market and works with you to the extent that you can make enough to where you don't feel pressured into trades or circumstances because you "have to" make a living. The pressure to provide can be the most motivating yet disastrous thing if you don't manage the conflict properly. This is something that is rarely talked about in many of the glory stories of traders who've made their own fortunes. But my guess is that all of them had to deal with this conflict if trading was their only source of revenue, whether they realized it or not.

S11-2: What helped you get through your learning curve the most: trial and error, trading books, a mentor, or something else?

Minervini: All of the above. Mostly, analyzing my past trades and gaining an understanding of what I was doing wrong over and over again. Once I found the common denominators, then it was just a matter of building up those weaknesses to strengths.

Ryan: Most of it was my own trial and error. Only I knew exactly what I was thinking at the time of a trade, and only I could really examine where my mistakes were made. You can get some guidance from a more successful trader and learn from trading books, but in the end, you have to internalize the rules that work for you in the market.

Zanger: It would have to be a combination of several books and my AIQ charting program. *How to Make Money in Stocks* has to be at the top of my list, with *Reminiscences of a Stock Operator* being up there too. These are must-reads for all traders and investors.

Ritchie II: I would say that all of the above helped me greatly. I would sum up my influences in the following order: faith, people, and practice.

Faith: I am a pretty unapologetic follower of Jesus. If you're asking, "What the heck does this have to do with trading?," for me it has everything to do with trading, because my identity is not in what I do or what I excel at, but in my faith. This gives me a tremendous amount of freedom to fail, which I think is central to any amount of success I may achieve. In addition, it's tough to fail if I'm truly doing what I feel called to do with whatever gifts and talents I've received, as they're ultimately not for my own glorification. There's still a tension here, as I want to be able to leave trading someday if I feel led to do so without second thoughts to pursue other endeavors, as I want to be a slave to nothing but His will for me.

People: I would be nowhere in terms of skill or wisdom without the influences of some key people. First and foremost would be my father, Mark Ritchie ("Mark the greater," as he's known in smaller circles). He gave me my first bit of capital to trade and the confidence to stick with it in addition to so many other things that I can't mention briefly, but he should get most of the credit. Mark Minervini, the man himself and his work, has greatly influenced a good deal of my stock trading, and Peter Brandt has greatly helped me better understand the guts of statistics as it applies to trading and specifically weathering drawdowns. Lastly I've been blessed with an incredible wife who has been massively supportive even when we had no money, as well as incredible friends and family who are too many to mention.

Practice: Successful trading is a result of practice. You learn how and what to practice by studying—studying the markets themselves, your trading results, and others who've been successful, as well as studying and pursuing how to improve yourself. My recommended reading list would be tough, but in regard to the markets specifically I'd say:

- *Reminiscences of a Stock Operator* by Edwin Lefèvre
- *Trade Like a Stock Market Wizard* by Mark Minervini
- *How to Trade in Stocks* by Jesse Livermore
- *How to Make Money in Stocks* by William O'Neil

- Anything and everything by Jack Schwager
- *Pit Bull* by Marty Schwartz

For personal improvement in regard to faith or psychology or for anyone wanting to take a walk on the wild side of what I hope to shape my soul and character, I'd recommend:

- *The New Testament*
- *Oikonomics* by Mike Breen and Ben Sternke
- *My Utmost for His Highest* by Oswald Chambers
- *Searching for God Knows What* by Donald Miller

S11-3: How important do you think it is to have a mentor in order to become successful?

Minervini: If your mentor is good, it can be extremely important and a pathway to learning the skills you need. It can shorten the learning curve and teach you things that you may never have learned on your own. But remember, practice only makes perfect if you're practicing the right things. So choose who teaches you carefully. A mentor should have already accomplished what you're trying to attain. I never could understand how someone could think he or she could learn how to make a million dollars from someone who never earned a million dollars. I even know a financial planner who previously went bankrupt! How absurd is that?

Ryan: Having a mentor could help save some time in focusing on the right things to look for, but you can also do it on your own. It might be harder and take longer, but it can be done alone through self-examination and through books or semi-nars from successful investors.

Zanger: That really depends on the mentor. Most of what I see out there is more self-hype than substance, and of course this will lead you into bankruptcy in no time. But if you are lucky enough to find a seasoned mentor with a great track record, that person is going to catapult you to the next level and beyond.

Ritchie II: I think having a good mentor or even mentors is priceless, as I previously alluded to. I strongly believe in the proverb that "wisdom is found in the counsel of many," so that we shouldn't often be content with what we think we know but always be willing to learn from those more experienced in knowledge and practice than ourselves.

S11-4: What was the most important "aha" moment in your trading career?

Minervini: When I finally realized that with correct risk management, I didn't have to find stocks that doubled and tripled to achieve triple-digit returns. I realized that I could trade smaller moves and still get huge returns, and more importantly, I could do it consistently. It's all about risk versus reward and turnover. That's the holy grail.

Ryan: The moment I studied the trades I made from my first year and realized what I was doing wrong. That is when I said I am only going to buy this one setup and not care about anything else. That is when it all started to work.

Zanger: That came in October 1997 when I was reading an oil index chart that created a key reversal bar one day after a strong summer run in stocks. I noted this reversal bar one evening and thought to myself that since this index was leading the market, this reversal bar may mean that the market has topped. Sure as the sun goes down every night, the market plunged from there, and my positions got smoked! I will never forget this moment or its results to my portfolio.

To this day, I'm still quick to get out of the market when I see potentially bearish charts or daily bars. And while I'm often right and safe on an early call, I can still be wrong, though that memory has served me well over these last few decades. Remember, you can always get back in.

Ritchie II: One of my biggest aha moments was when I realized the power of compounding a good idea or approach. I realized that it was possible to really grow money if you managed the downside and stuck with a winning strategy.

S11-5: What are your top five trading rules?

Minervini:

1. Think risk first. Always trade with a stop loss and know where you're getting out before you get in.
2. Keep losses small and protect your breakeven point once you attain a decent profit.
3. Never risk more than you expect to gain.
4. Never average down.
5. Know the truth about your trading—study your results regularly.

Ryan:
1. Cut your losses and keep them small.
2. Be extremely disciplined.
3. Trade smaller if you have a number of losses in a row.
4. Never let a good gain turn into a loss.
5. Move money from your losers to your winners.

Zanger:
1. Never let a stock get below what you paid for it.
2. Never chase a stock that is up more than 3–5% above its pivot or breakout area.
3. Avoid options.
4. Reduce position size after a good move up.
5. Hang on to those winners and let go of the laggards.

Ritchie II:
1. Always trade with a plan, specifically one that evaluates risk in every possible way for an individual position as well as your entire portfolio.
2. Always reduce trading size after a big loss or losing period.
3. Shift capital to ideas and strategies that are working and reduce it from ones that aren't.
4. Guard your emotions with equal value to the way you guard your capital.
5. Bring your "A" game every day.

S11-6: Why does the average investor fail to achieve big performance?

Minervini: The following are some of the main reasons traders fail to attain big performance in the stock market:

- Use poor selection criteria.
- Don't cut losses—most common mistake.
- Add to losing positions—the number one reason traders blow up.
- Don't protect profits—they let decent gains turn into losses (very common mistake).
- Don't know the truth about their trading—they fail to conduct periodic post-analysis.
- Don't commit to a strategy—they experience what we call style drift and give up too soon (also very common).
- Have a breakdown in discipline—even if they have rules, eventually they break them.

Ryan: Either they don't have the right emotional makeup to invest, or they won't study their mistakes and correct them. If someone employs a growth stock strategy, there are a lot of books from great traders like Mark Minervini, William O'Neil, and others that lay out the right rules for them, but it is the average investor's responsibility to make it work.

Zanger: The average investor usually has a full-time job and likely kids and many other distractions that consume his or her time. This leaves little time to do the homework and chart pattern interpretation required to rise above just average.

Ritchie II: Average investors certainly don't understand enough about the market to begin with to have consistent big performances. Even if they did though, there would be an even smaller number who had the knowledge as well as the discipline required to consistently follow through with doing the right things. As my father eloquently points out in his recent book *My Trading Bible*, knowledge and talent are great, but "discipline gets the job done."

S11-7: What advice would you give to a new trader?

Minervini: Get a good role model, someone who has already accomplished what you're aspiring to do. Don't get discouraged if you don't perform well in the first few years; it takes time to learn how to trade. Realize that you're going to make a huge number of mistakes and that you need to learn from those mistakes; they are your best teacher. You have to take action and gain experience. Come up with a plan and take action. Any plan is better than no plan.

You must be willing to put in the work and own your failures. Then you can own your success. Understand that there are no "secrets." For most traders, the biggest challenge is sticking to a strategy and maintaining discipline. Most traders would fail even if you gave them a successful strategy because they can't commit to the learning curve and make it through the difficult times. They lose confidence in the strategy, and they lose confidence in their own abilities.

Ryan: Read all the material put out by William O'Neil, *Investor's Business Daily*, MarketSmith, and Mark Minervini. Study it and start investing. Even if it is a few hundred dollars, get started. You will learn a lot with your first investment. Learn from your mistakes and correct them. Never give up, and keep trying. With enough effort, your returns could make a tremendous difference in your future.

Zanger: Read the books I've noted previously. Then start trading lightly without margin or options until you can put together solid gains for six to nine months and have lived through a market correction as well as can spot a market or stock reversal.

Ritchie II: I would keep it very simple and tell new traders to focus on what I call the "three Ms": a market, a method, and myself. If you get all three working together, you'll be successful.

Better Investing.

Minervini Private Access

A Click Away

www.minervini.com

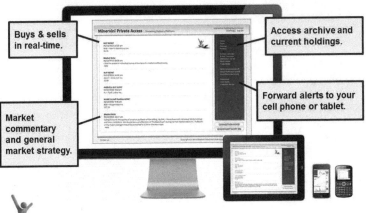

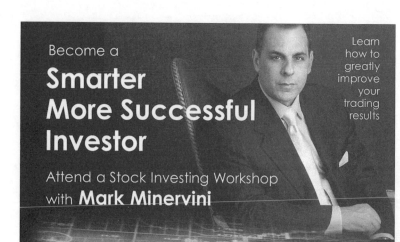

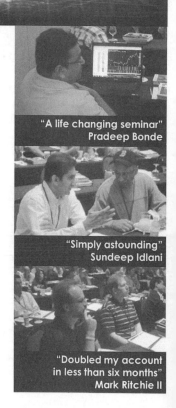